# THE LEGEND OF RIVER MAHAY

Based on a true Alaska
adventure story of love, survival
and triumph over adversity.

## DEBORAH COX WOOD
### WITH CHRISTOPHER BATIN

*Enjoy –*
*Deb Wood*

ISBN 978-1-59433-057-5

Library of Congress Catalog Card Number: 2007928274

Copyright 2007 by Triple D, LLC
—First Edition—

Photos courtesy of Chris Batin, Steve and Sharon Mahay,
Evan Swensen, and Deborah and Nicole Wood. Devils
Canyon photos courtesy of Adela Jackson/Alaska Angler
Photobank. Cover photo courtesy of Evan Swensen, Publi-
cation Consultants. Cover design by Tracy Holland, Thala
Graphics, LLC and Hal Gage, Gage Photo Graphics.

Manufactured in the United States of America.

# Dedication

This book is dedicated to
Jack and Rose Yukon,
wilderness soul mates.

# Acknowledgements

Traveling all over the world brings plenty of opportunities to enjoy the gifts of nature, but each one of 15 or more yearly visits to Alaska confirmed that I was hopelessly in love with this land. Her beauty, charm, and the inner strength of its residents have captured my heart and I return often.

I want to acknowledge my special family: My husband, Breck, who loved Alaska and this story as much as I did, but passed away before its completion, making the telling of it more precious, but bitter-sweet. Our daughters Nicole and Dana; Dana's husband Jesse Mace; and especially Mom, Nana Zella Cox. Each one loves Alaska as much as I do, and whenever possible we return to experience more amazing adventures.

There were many who helped at home so I could travel, such as my partners and friends, Walt Kelley and Maureen Gallagher; along with our staff at Heritage Title, especially Cindy, my assistant, and her husband, Billy, who took care of many tedious details. Thank you also to all supportive friends at William E. Wood & Associates.

Special love and gratitude is given to Sharon and Steve Mahay. They allowed me to tell their story; were tireless with the research and re-writes; and graciously tolerant of a 'novel' approach. This project began with our families being mere acquaintances, but sealed us forever as good friends. They are the treasures from these Alaska adventures.

I also want to express gratitude to all the Mahay's Riverboat Service employees and family members for their interest in this project, by allowing their stories to be taped, and giving me permission and the liberty to tell about the legends that surround them in my own way.

Finally, deep appreciation is offered to the professionals who helped to better tell the story, especially Chris Batin, who spent as much time helping me fine tune this book as I spent in writing the original manuscript, making it, as he says, "a classic that sings." Other professional cheerleaders and mentors are: John Aliano, Marthy Johnson, Larry Ka-niut, Alice Widman, and my patient publisher, Evan Swensen. Many hours were spent rewriting and exploring how to present this material better in order to honor Steve Mahay and his life.

All these individuals have been subject to the frustrations of my writing and living styles, summed up by this quote from the author Melinda Haynes: "Forget all the rules. Forget about being published. Write for yourself and celebrate writing."

# Contents

# Foreword

Throughout the history of pioneering, there is always one person with suitable dimensions of spirit and character who stands out among the rest. He or she is the one leading the nomadic tribes across Beringia or Mongolia, standing against wind and wave on the helm of a Viking explorer ship, or taking the point on horseback to lead a wagon train into the American West. Anyone destined to be a pioneer must have broad shoulders and know how to lead, but more importantly, how to serve.

Alaska also has its own requirements for those who would pioneer its wilderness. Survival requires knowing the old ways of woodsmanship and self-sufficiency. The would-be pioneer must possess drive and focus, yet possess a sensitivity that respects all things in nature. The pioneer must also be able to survive the toughest conditions and stand there, undeterred, or if fallen, get up and keep going, no matter what.

*The Legend of River Mahay* is Dr. Deborah Cox Wood's celebration of a lifestyle that describes the remarkable exploits and adventures of just such an individual; Steve Mahay—a man who is as big as all of Alaska, with a life story that will keep you spellbound in the spirit of the Last Frontier.

I first met Steve Mahay in 1979. He was back then as he is now, a man who is the epitome of adventure and spirit, suited for the river bottomlands he so dearly loves. In those early years, however, he was just beginning to turn those river and outdoor skills into a business, and I remember he worked hard at it. At the time, I was working as editor-in-chief for *Alaska Outdoors* magazine, and Steve was a regular advertiser in that publication. He always had a new fishing spot or news to tell me, and often invited me to explore new waters with him. He knew that keeping his message in the forefront of our readership would help build his business. As I got to know the man, the business relationship turned into friendship because he sincerely cared about people and the resources in his beloved Talkeetna River country.

Some of my favorite memories were when he'd pilot the boat on numerous trips on the Talkeetna and Susitna rivers. I listened to him talk about the area, pan for gold, and interact with wildlife. I often observed him giving the best fishing holes to someone else. He would still catch more fish, albeit secretly around the bend and out of sight. He prided himself as a flyfisher, yet was humble in his angling skills and achievements. Most importantly, he treated each customer who was all thumbs with a spinning reel (and he had his share) with patience and respect.

Few can match his riverboat piloting skills and experience. He doesn't drive a boat; he wears it. I've seen it, and it's a custom fit like no other. I've seen him work as a fishing guide, yet put the fishing aside and become an on-stream counselor, helping men and women with their lives and building relationships. All this is the very crux of what being a legend is all about; kindness and compassion interspersed with exploits more fascinating than Paul Bunyan and more benevolent than Johnny Appleseed.

He'd invite me to dinner at his home and would explain the complexities of running a riverboat operation. I listened as he spoke from real-world experience with authority and confidence that would later serve him well in business and the outdoor worlds. I saw an entrepreneur who was more than a man of the mountains and rivers. This man was going places. That was 28 years ago. It's safe to say the man, and the legend, are here to stay.

But this is more than a book about a man. Deborah captures the essence of the celebration of the Alaska way of life, its characters and eccentrics, its disappointments and its dreams of everyman who wants to survive adversity and know what it feels like to be the one triumphantly standing in the end. *The Legend of River Mahay* is about the many levels of survival, of people who take the most severe punishment nature can dish out. Although hammered down, each one still rises with enough breath and pride of spirit to shout, "I am undefeated!" This book is about an undying heart, the search for hope, a love story, and of survival and triumph over adversity, all mixed into one. It is about Alaska pioneers who not only never give up, but who also choose to live this way and no other.

But perhaps most of all, this is a story about a man who wants to know what is always on the other side of the ridge, and who does what it takes to get there. His story is about lifestyle and values, of choices and consequences. He pioneered the route to climbing the

Everest in his profession, and boldly journeyed where no man has gone before. He did it right, and is still doing it.

Deborah also does a superb job in merging fact with a sprinkling of fiction, or *faction* as we call it in writing circles. It is a writing style that not only informs, but also entertains, while still keeping to the accomplishments and truth of the man, the myth, and the legend.

She then proceeds to take us deeper into the heart and soul of the man, to that place where legends often don't go and life is not always rosy. There are mistakes. Divorce. Triumphs. Self-doubts.

She weaves a story that is complex, yet as subtle as an Alaska autumn. On the surface, it is indeed beautiful to the eye. But the literary sourdough sees another message hidden beneath the leafy, colorful prose.

*The Legend of River Mahay* is more than just a book of true-to-life achievements, interviews and experiences. It is a celebration of many things Alaska. Some might see Steve Mahay fighting off aggressive grizzly bears. But as Sun Tzu writes in *The Art of War*, "You must see the subtle and notice the hidden to be victorious."

I urge you to embrace this view when reading *The Legend of River Mahay*, for there is meaning here far greater than conflict between man and bear, or man against river. This book is an allegorical tale of the struggle all Alaska pioneers endure. Take the adversity with the bears and substitute fear, discouragement, isolation, failure, and hardships that all pioneers endure to survive, succeed and evolve in the wilderness. Perhaps the bears are the anthropomorphic realization of nature interacting with a man who is one with the Alaska wilds. The story is open to your interpretation, except for one aspect. Steve Mahay is as much a part of nature as a raindrop that falls into the ocean. Once the raindrop enters the sea, it loses its form and becomes one with its surroundings. Such is River Mahay in the Alaska wilderness. The two are separate in form, yet when joined, are inseparable.

The frontier life is also about relationships. Deborah introduces characters with their tales of love, animosity, jealousy, courage, toughness, true grit and heart. She doesn't do this because it reads better, but rather, is relaying a variety of qualities and stories of real-life Alaskans. I've seen and met most of them. I've been there. I know.

To be an Alaskan is an honor that is coveted by those who appreciate its meaning and implications. Deborah teaches us that being an Alaskan is a rite of passage, of survivorship, of pride in belonging to the people who individually and collectively make it The Last Frontier.

Deborah spent countless hours and dollars immersing herself in the myriad lifestyles of these residents, their personal and professional lives. She accompanied River and Sharon into remote areas, hiked the trails and experienced the rivers. She listened to their hopes and dreams, disappointments, triumphs, and adversities. Deborah absorbed it all and created a blueprint for this book. This was no easy task, for in order for her to pull this off so effectively, she had to see with more than the eyes and listen with more than the ears in her head. She listened and saw with the senses of her heart. As a result, she captured the essence of what makes Alaskans tick as her subject, River Mahay, is so fond of saying. She is as tough and resilient as any Alaskan, and only a person such as she could write this book. You can take the person out of Alaska, but you can't take Alaska out of the person, and this aptly applies to Deborah and her book, one that is destined to be a welcome addition to Alaska literature.

*The Legend of River Mahay* is a classic I will enjoy reading again and again, not only because it celebrates the achievements and accomplishments of a very dear friend, but also because author Deborah Cox Wood is a literary guide extraordinaire. She reveals to us that being an Alaskan is not just a name, but rather, a celebration of an adventure lifestyle, a dream that all of us have within us.

It is my most sincere wish that you also sample this lifestyle in person or through the pages of this book.

Christopher Batin
Editor and Publisher
Alaska Angler/Alaska Hunter Publications
www.AlaskaAngler.com
Fairbanks, Alaska

# Preface

The characters and stories in this book are true, except for The Big One, Demon Eyes and Chet Bastian. All three represent the creative imagination of the author, subject to the tolerant indulgences of Steve and Sharon Mahay, and perfectly explained by Chris Batin in the Foreword as "merging fact with a sprinkling of fiction, or *faction*."

It is true, however, that the way of the wilderness is not fair, when kill or be killed can be a daily encounter. Because of the wondrous and magical nature of Alaska, the author is certain The Big One must exist, at least in the recesses of her mind, and of course he would befriend such a legendary man as River Mahay.

## Introduction
# Legend Discovered

"Is it true it only costs one dollar to check my luggage for the whole day?" I asked.

It was hard to believe that in 2005, one dollar had enough value to end my fitful battle with a piece of luggage. I had just dragged the Christian Dior suitcase across the gravel parking lot. The wheels were caked with mud and stopped rotating. I was nearly in tears after pulling the heavy object that wouldn't roll, while trying to maintain some dignity with the passing traffic.

"That's right," said the cheerful attendant and all the people standing around nodded. Their smiles and exuberance reminded me of watching a television commercial. The clerk came out from behind the desk and led me into the back storage area where several suitcases had been abandoned by other travelers who must have found themselves in similar circumstances.

I gratefully paid my dollar, and left the storage area for the front part of the building that held books, gifts, memorabilia, and many interesting items to purchase for friends and family. I was also hopeful to find research material for a novel I had been writing about a female helicopter pilot in Alaska.

I picked up several items and one book in particular caught my eye—*Cheating Death, Amazing Survival Stories of Alaska*. As I stood in line to pay for my new treasures, and was thumbing through the chapters of the book, someone asked, "Do you want me to autograph that for you?"

I quickly looked up into the handsome, tanned face of a man of slim build who was wearing a jacket with "Mahay's Riverboat Service" embroidered on the front. He wore jeans, a white shirt and not surprisingly—muddy boots. The little bit of gray peeking through his sandy brown hair convinced me that he was older than he looked. I would have thought him to be in his early 40s, but was surprised to learn that he was in his late 50s. He stood with a pen in hand ready to do the honor of signing his name. His smile was engaging. I couldn't resist as I eagerly handed him the book and asked if he had written it.

"No," he said and laughed. "But I'm Chapter Eight. I've wanted to write my life's story, but haven't had the time." He signed his name and handed the book back to me as I finished paying. Then he disappeared behind the desk and went back to work.

I looked at the signature on Chapter Eight, then turned to the clerk who had been assisting me and asked, "Who is Steve Mahay?"

"He's the owner and founder of this business, and the one who appears in all the pictures around the store," she answered.

I spent the next hour browsing the many newspaper articles and commendation plaques about the amazing feats performed on the river by this man. I felt honored and excited to have met him.

I learned from the articles that he was the first man to successfully navigate a jetboat up the treacherous waters inside Devils Canyon. Since I was a helicopter pilot, I felt an instant affinity toward him when I saw the picture of a helicopter carrying one of his jetboats out of the canyon. The more I read, the more fascinated I became.

He had saved many lives on the river and received a commendation from the governor. There were certificates showing he was elected to prestigious boards that made decisions about the area's tourist industry and growth. It appeared that Steve Mahay had been taking people on fishing tours for over 30 years. He had lived in the wilderness, built his own cabins with only an axe, survived the elements and had exciting encounters with bears. A real-life, modern-day Daniel Boone-type character. From a writer's perspective, I was hooked.

Thanks to the unfortunate demise of my suitcase wheels, I had stumbled across a fascinating man whose story shouted to be told. This accidental meeting of Steve "River" Mahay introduced me to the classic tale you are about to read and convinced me that there are still heroes to be found in America.

I have often pondered how legends and folklore are mixed with shades of truth. The underlying stories are often real and people love to hear them as reminders that mankind has the potential for achieving nobility and integrity. In fact, these tales frequently inspire readers with the possibilities of experiencing heroism in their own lives through the characters described on the pages of books.

On one hand, the old glory cowboy days were full of gunslingers who sought to bring down men with legendary status in their own time—a sort of David and Goliath scenario where the underdog achieved his own new status by removing the *obstacle*. Many such men chased legends such as Wyatt Earp and the notorious Doc Holliday, celebrated gamblers and sharpshooters, because they aspired to be famous even if it meant the taking of another man's life.

On the other hand, there are men and women who do not seek glory or shortcut status to fame, but who are driven by the motivation to do the right thing for the right reason. These are rare individuals, about whom history books are written, and their stories are shared around campfires or at night next to a child's bed. The storyteller or parent is hopeful that the tales will inspire within the listener a desire to be noble and strong like the hero.

I am excited to say that I discovered that there is such a man, noble and living out his dreams, a modern legend in a magical place that really exists. His name is Steve Mahay. He carved out a life for himself and others on the rivers that run by a little village called Talkeetna in the amazing state of Alaska.

To the reader, who may or may not have a chance to visit Alaska's glorious wilderness in person, this book introduces you to many of River Mahay's riverboat adventures, near-death occurrences and exciting bear encounters.

Each year, Mahay's Riverboat Service staff introduces thousands of tourists to the many wonders of the Talkeetna, Susitna, and Chulitna rivers. And if you keep an eye open and ask around, chances are good you'll see River Mahay piloting a boat, running errands, or overseeing repairs. But unlike many legends, this one is approachable. Stop by, say hello, and ask for a story or autograph. I promise, you won't be disappointed.

Deborah Cox Wood
Talkeetna, Alaska
May, 2007
DrDCWood@aol.com
www.SettlingwithPower.com

# Chapter One
# The Legend

In the 1970s, like pioneers of old, River (who was still known as Steve in those days) Mahay loaded up his yellow Volkswagen Super Beatle and headed northwest to escape the influences of a society which he felt softened a man and lulled him into complacency; a society that made him forget what was important in life.

He began his journey by leaving Saratoga Springs, New York, where he had grown up working on a farm with his parents, two brothers and two sisters. They were simple folk, raising poultry and vegetables. He had managed to spend time trout fishing and hunting in his youth, oftentimes at the expense of school classes, but graduated from Schulerville High School in 1966. He soon joined the Peace Corps, answering a call to serve by John F. Kennedy, who originally formed the Corps, and spent time in India teaching agriculture to starving people.

When River returned home from the difficult lifestyles he had witnessed in India, he realized there was more to his American Dream than just earning money, and more to life than pitching hay and shoveling manure. He craved a life filled with meaningful adventure. Some of his heroes—Lewis and Clark, Davy Crockett, and Daniel Boone—had contributed much to the early days of this country. Virginia, Kentucky, Tennessee and the Far West, however, had been tamed, settled, and changed forever. Was there a frontier remaining for a modern adventurer?

River decided to head north to Alaska, the last American wilderness. The skills he learned on the family farm and the steely toughness acquired from working the barren fields of India, had tempered him in the fire of experience and prepared him for what lie ahead. He packed an axe, hunting rifles, beans, flour, a bucksaw and a small fortune of $240, said goodbye to the world he knew, and prepared to embrace a new life in The Great Land.

River believed that living in nature was an opportunity for a man to test himself, see what he was made of, and discover his limitations. He would push himself to the edge: Succeed or be beaten down trying.

Thinking of his heroes of old, and in honor of their resilience, River staked out 10 acres. The land offered spruce trees for building a cabin and high ground for protection. There was a river for traveling that also provided a good source of water and fish, and a magnificent view of Mount McKinley to inspire the spirit. He reminisced:

> *When I first arrived in Alaska in 1972, there were about 100 trappers, prospectors, and gold miners who lived in Talkeetna. Tourism was not even a factor. Some hunters came through, as well as fishermen, but we didn't see the general tourists seen today. It used to be, if we saw a tourist, we'd run and get our hunting binoculars because we wanted to see what a tourist really looked like up close.*

With no idea of where all this would take him, River built a home 10 miles from the nearest town. It had no road access and was near a well-traveled and active bear path. He was going to test himself to the limits. He explained his choices by saying, "Whatever I do, I'm consumed. If you're not going to do it with all you've got, why bother?"

His mother, Shirley Mahay, instilled strong work ethics in River at an early age. She insisted that an individual could be or have anything the world had to offer, as long as he was willing to work hard to get it. River was going to put his mother's words to the test with the wilderness experience.

One warm afternoon, River Mahay was driving through a dense part of forest near Talkeetna, going about five mph on a bad road. Suddenly, a cow moose and her calf shot through a turn in the road at full gallop and headed straight for his pickup. Seconds later, River knew why. A huge grizzly bear soon rounded the same turn in hot pursuit, mouth open and kicking up gravel as he gained ground on the calf.

The cow and calf shot past a mere six feet from his truck door, but River wasn't concerned with them. The grizzly loomed large and intimidating through the windshield. River knew the calf didn't have a chance unless he intervened, *now!*

He flung open the driver's door and used the open window frame to quickly get a rest for his .45 Long Colt. He found the bear in his sights, lead it and squeezed slowly as he kept leading. The shot slammed into the dirt in front of the charging bear.

The loud muzzle blast and dirt spray from the bullet's impact stopped the bear as if it had run into an invisible wall. The bruin stood up slowly, towering above the truck, weaving and head-swaying from being cheated out of a meal. Its massive head faced River and beady black eyes met his gaze. River steadied his sights on the bear, and his finger tightened on the trigger. The bruin's dirt-covered, wet nose sniffed the air. The hair on Steve's arms bristled as both predators waited for the other to make the first move. After an eternity of seconds, the grizzly dropped down to all fours. Its muscular, lumbering hulk disappeared into the thick brush, dividing it as easily as an axe splits wood.

River knew he had saved the moose and calf at the risk of his own life. He thought of his old adage, which generally applied to humans: *When someone is in trouble, you drop whatever you are doing and help. Your hesitation can make the difference between life and death.*

His instinct to help was not just for man, but every creature when he could. The eye-to-eye encounter with the grizzly had left him with an odd feeling of familiarity, yet he couldn't recall seeing this bear before now. One thing was certain: This grizzly had to be the notorious and much discussed, Big One. He had never before seen such a large bear.

Still standing beside the open truck door, he reflected on the appalling wounds of the victims he had encountered in one of his many jobs as a community emergency medical technician. *A mauling is always a brutal tragedy. The Big One could have finished me off with one flick of its paw. I wonder why he didn't.*

What a false sense of protection he felt. He climbed into his pickup and continued down the bumpy road. He thought of the irony in how humans felt safe behind their protective metal and wooden doors. *Never seen a door or window that a bear couldn't get through, if he had such a mind.*

The Big One could have broken the windshield with one powerful swat. River shook off the last vestiges of an adrenaline rush, joking that perhaps the bear had met his match. Realistically though, River knew the bear could have easily attacked, and the consequences would have been tragic for either one.

Having lived in the Alaska Bush for over 30 years, he was well aware of the unpredictable behavior of bears. The decision to attack or not was totally the bear's choice and there was a real possibility that he might make a different decision next time. *If there was a next time.*

River Mahay had lots of bear experience. He lived in this wilderness by choice and had faced death many times. He had developed skills and muscles to carve out a business in the middle of nowhere, while dealing simultaneously with daily survival. Suddenly returning to normal and feeling calm, he realized that it had been a long time since he had thought about home being anyplace except Alaska. *The wilderness could be unforgiving to the weak. It was fortunate that my first encounter with The Big One was without disaster. Except,* he laughed, *The Big One didn't get a baby moose meal.*

He ruefully wished he had gotten a camera shot of the gigantic bear to use for advertising or bragging rights, but there had been no time. He had to take another kind of shot.

River's business entertained thousands of visitors each summer and it was a big contributor to the area's economy. He'd helped place the little village of Talkeetna solidly on the map.

When traveling by himself or with others while trapping, fishing, hunting or boating, he was never far from the possibility of running into bears. And now he had seen The Big One. That bear was becoming a nuisance to his family and community. Some were really afraid, and he felt responsible for the safety of many who counted on him.

# Chapter Two
# The Big One

River recognized that eventually The Big One would have to be eliminated because he was showing up in populated areas and too close to home. The Big One was named by the natives and locals in the Denali area because of his size. Few people had ever seen him up close, but each time the tale was told, he became larger. The ones who had encountered him and were without physical or emotional scars knew they were fortunate. Some said, and River agreed, that The Big One was over 1,000 pounds, and stood at least 12 feet tall. If he didn't want to be seen, he wouldn't, but a person could be sure he was near. Just observe the dogs. They wouldn't move, except to softly whimper, as their hair prickled and stood up on their backs. The intruder could feel the bear observing him and knew that if the bear chose him for dinner, there wasn't much that he could do to prevent it.

The grizzly has no natural predator except man with the proper weapon. Stories abound of armed men shooting numerous bullets into the massive bodies of charging grizzlies. The bullets failed to dispatch the bears before the bruins exacted revenge on them.

According to bear experts, grizzlies are highly evolved and intelligent animals that learn to change their behavior based on an experience or consequence. This humanistic trait has caused some men to carelessly let down their guard, but grizzlies in the wild seldom do. It's important to the survival of both man and grizzly to always remember that each is dangerous to the other. History has proven fatal for either one who forgot that detail.

In 2003, the disaster of the late Timothy Treadwell made the headlines. He was a well-known grizzly-bear advocate who spent more than a dozen summers living in the Alaska Bush observing and researching "his bears," naming them, filming them, and refusing to heed warnings from the experts. He believed he was on a personal mission as their protector and predicted that he might die for his zeal, but was willing to take that chance. *Carry a gun or at the very least a can of bear spray* was the expert advice he stubbornly declined to observe.

He refused to hurt bears in any way. He brought his girlfriend, a kindred biologist, on his last two trips and that final summer they camped on a known bear trail. When the supply plane flew in for its regular delivery, the pilot saw that something was amiss. From overhead he could see a bear near the tent, eating what he thought was a human torso. It was later learned that Timothy and his girlfriend had been eaten alive. A tape had been left ominously running and the sounds of their horrendous fates were recorded for all time.

Also in the Denali area, there was a young man who was innocently fishing with his friends when attacked under ordinary, therefore unpredictable, circumstances. He was walking in a very popular fishing area, laughing and jovial, minding his own business, when a huge grizzly charged out of the woods and mauled him severely. The young man lived, but the facial scars of the experience would endure forever. Everyone who witnessed the unfortunate incident agreed it had to be The Big One.

The public consensus was that this bear was angry with humans, or maybe just wanted to teach them a lesson. This king of bears could do whatever he wanted, whenever and to whomever he chose. No one knew why The Big One attacked that particular young man. By the time the shock wore off and rifles were aimed in his direction, he had disappeared. They say he didn't even run, but rather just sauntered away, his huge hips swaying back and forth, as though mocking them.

This danger does not run in just one direction. There are many warning signs posted throughout Alaska, with the message in bold print: *A Fed Bear is a Dead Bear*. Well-meaning-but-ignorant visitors often present food to a bear, or leave food exposed where the bear may help himself or try to hand it off to the bear as a thrill. When bears become adapted to non-natural food sources such as garbage cans, bird feeders, dog food, dumps, or any other means by which food is associated with humans, they may put themselves in harm's way by approaching people who do not understand their intent. They will be killed by authorities that reluctantly put bears down as a last resort due to people's unthinking actions.

Human presence in the wilderness consistently upsets the gentle balance of nature. Even hikers might startle a dining moose and inadvertently cause it to jump in the river. If there is a calf in tow, it could follow and drown. If a bear were nearby he would go after the calf, because to a bear, according to River Mahay, a calf is nothing more than apple pie.

To the locals, The Big One was an unpredictable, savage beast. His presence was another tragedy waiting to happen. He was nothing more than a monster that enjoyed unprovoked savagery in populated areas where bears generally did not venture. People were supposed to be safe from bear attacks under certain circumstances. But as Echo Sackett said in Louis L'Amour's *Ride the River*,

> *We live in a wild country, sir. I know folks who think all wild things are sweet and cuddly, but they've never come into a henhouse after a weasel has been there. He can drink the blood of one or two, but often as not, he'll kill every one of them. Wolves will do it in a pen of lambs, too. There are savage beasts in the world, and men who are just as savage.*

Where would The Big One strike next, and who would be the unsuspecting victim? His existence among the inhabitants of this beautiful wilderness area seemed to simulate the proverbial battle between good and evil. The bear was there first, some might argue, therefore technically having the rights to the place. But humans being humans always seemed to put the lie to this logic, intruding where even the most beautiful and breathtaking of indigenous creatures would become quarry. Maybe The Big One was just evening the score.

# Chapter Three
# Wedding Disruption

The wedding of Jacque and Lisa, both River's employees, took place just outside town near a stand of trees on the riverbank. The participants in the ceremony looked out of character because they wore formal tuxedos instead of T-shirts and blue jeans. Weapons were left in the vehicles.

The preacher was always uncomfortable without his handgun holstered to his hip, but this was a wedding ceremony and not a place for guns.

The concluding words were intoned without interruption from man or beast with, "I now pronounce you husband and wife."

And the groom gladly leaned over and kissed his new bride, while everyone clapped and cheered.

The preacher was none other than River Mahay. In Alaska, every resident is licensed to perform one marriage ceremony. Although River was ordained and had done a fair amount of preaching from the pulpit of the local Christian church, he had no formal training to be a preacher of the Word of God. But 32 years of living in this last frontier, along with certain unique state laws, gave him the necessary authority.

River had spent many long, dark, and extremely cold winters of 20 to 60 below studying The Word, and he was able to go head-to-head with any formally educated preacher over what The Good Book said.

At the wedding reception, River scanned the room filled with happy friends and family, and then rested on Sharon, his very own bride of five short and wonderful months. His eyes embraced her face as delicately as morning dew caresses a blossoming rose. She glanced back at him and smiled, making his heart swell in his chest. He was surprised she still had that effect on him and hoped it would last forever, recalling the first time he saw her in Talkeetna, browsing in his store.

He had overheard her speaking with a woman that he later learned to be her mother, recognizing the familiar accent of the place he had left so many winters ago, New York. Immediately taken with her beauty, he quickly noticed she wasn't wearing a wedding ring. Since it wasn't there claiming her for someone else, River had fallen head over heels in a matter of moments.

His instincts told him she was right for him, and his gut was never wrong. He had been trained in the wild, fine-tuned by the very fires of nature. He remembered being overcome by a sense of urgency to know her, and recognized that he only had a few moments before she walked out the door and out of his life. He approached her and smiled, not knowing what to say. Her twinkling eyes and beautiful smile invited him to forge on. She made it easy for him to speak with her. They idly chattered in surface talk, finding common ground in stories of the riverboats of Niagara Falls.

Eventually, fearing that he would lose the opportunity to find out more about her, he offered her his Devils Canyon video in exchange for her email address. She willingly accepted and later admitted that she never expected to hear from him again. She told him it had been a pleasant surprise to discover she had mail from him and for a short while, the Internet had been their only way to communicate and explore each other. River wanted more than anything to know what made her tick. Sharon wanted more than anything to tell him.

*She wanted to share her life with me*, he thought again, happily and glad that they were now together as husband and wife. It hadn't been easy to talk her into getting married. She had never married before and he knew that she held those vows sacred and would not make them lightly. He had wined and dined her for two years, on the Internet, phone and then later, planned trips. They had joyously traveled to the warmer climates of the world, and had enjoyed the voyage of discovering each other, sharing hopes, dreams, pains and disappointments. Each listened to the other from the heart and love grew. They had shared many interests: scuba diving, fine dining, boating, family, spirituality and meeting new people while forming new friends, together.

He smiled at her again and her lips formed the words, *I love you*, and he nodded, wishing they were alone. *It feels good to be alive.* It was Alaska that had brought Sharon to him and Alaska that allowed him to live out his wilderness dream.

Jacque and Lisa's wedding ceremony had taken place in a rustic setting near the Susitna River Lodge. There had been great concern over the weather. It had rained for a week prior, quit only an hour before, and was untraditionally warm for the season. *A good omen, if you believed in them,* he thought.

The men in the wedding felt like fish out of water as they squirmed and tugged at their rented, starched tuxedos. The women looked enchanting, especially Lisa, who wore a lovely traditional wedding dress, making the transformation from rustic to refined complete. It was September, and the tourist season was winding down, which was fortunate since most of the captains and employees of Mahay's Riverboat Service were either in the wedding or attending as guests.

The Lodge was in the village of Talkeetna, named after the Talkeetna River, an Indian name meaning "the joining of the rivers" or "plentiful river." It was a two-block-long town in the foothills of the massive mountain peak known as Mount McKinley, or Denali, meaning "The Great One."

There was once a plaque displayed in town that said the winter population for the small village was "378 People and One Grouch." Now it was more like 800, but they still claimed to have at least one grouch. If the tourists were counted, along with the spring and summer population of climbers, campers, and sightseers passing through on the way to Denali National Park, the number hovered in the tens of thousands.

Even with the season coming to an end, a few stragglers were still coming to town, eager to figure out what Alaska residents do all winter or to catch a view of the aurora borealis that danced, swirled and raced in multi-colored curtains across the winter sky.

Night was coming earlier and daylight would soon become a rare commodity. No one minded. Locals accepted these seasonal changes in the same manner as inhabitants of a large city in the Lower 48 accepted the traffic on the highway. What was—just was.

The locals loved the wintry weather. Some, like Sandi Mischenko, River's office manager, actually admitted that she lived for the winter and couldn't wait to begin planning for the fun, cold-weather activities, which were odd to outsiders or new residents. Active affairs such as the Wilderness Woman Contest, and of course, the Bachelor's Auction and Carhartt Ball astounded newcomers, along with some fair-weather activities like the Mountain Mother and Moose Dropping festivals.

Sandi's explanation of the events to the tourists brought serious chuckles. "Some of these events have been designed by the men in town to lure the women into staying through the winter."

The Talkeetna Chamber of Commerce advertised these exciting happenings as being "conducted in a spirit of good fun, but a sense of humor is highly recommended."

River's bride, Sharon, enjoyed being a part of the festivities, and was grateful to be readily accepted in the community. She strolled over to River and gently took his hand to walk the short distance to their car, to drive to the reception held at Sheldon Community Arts Hangar. Formerly it had been an airplane hangar at the end of the town's original airstrip that went right through the middle of town. Plenty of good food and drink would be found inside the old hangar. The residents knew that having the food outside might attract animals, especially bears.

River was reflecting about the troublesome bear. He felt preoccupied in constantly having to consider where he was and what he was up to.

"I've just about had it with the fear that is starting to build in Talkeetna over The Big One," he informed Sharon.

"I know," she agreed. "He has really started to affect the innocence of our little village. Being constantly on guard makes me think of New York City and worrying about a drive-by shooting."

They laughed at the analogy. Since Sharon had only been living in Alaska for five months, the Lower 48 lifestyle was still very real to her. She wondered how people up here lived with the constant fear of animal attacks.

River had lived in Alaska so long, he'd forgotten about the fear of violence from anything but animals and the elements, and those things didn't scare him, just kept him prepared.

"You know," he continued, "I never really thought of it before, but there doesn't seem much difference in the dangers of our two worlds, does there?"

"Not really," she agreed. "The two-footed bad guys or the four-footed creatures. Guess an animal is an animal."

"What are you two talking about?" Lisa and Jacque had strolled over to them without being noticed and interrupted their conversation. "You're not supposed to look happier than us today."

Everyone laughed and Sharon blushed.

She still felt like a newlywed, and was deeply in love with her mountain man. It hadn't been easy moving from the other side of the world and leaving all her friends and family behind. She was glad they were soon going to New York for a long visit.

"I'm not ready to become an instant sourdough, in addition to so many other subtle changes," she had informed River.

*Sourdough* is a term that describes someone who had spent a winter in Alaska. A more popular definition is someone who's been in Alaska long enough to become grumpy (or sour) but doesn't have enough money (or dough) to leave. There were longer versions of what it took to become a sourdough. Whatever it took, Sharon wasn't up to spending a winter in Alaska, at least not yet.

"That's okay. We only need one sourdough in this family," River said as he squeezed her hand. "Besides, we have a lot of marketing to do this winter in the Lower 48. You've got to get moving in your new job and earn your keep!"

"Slave driver," she said, playfully punching him in the arm. "Earn my keep, huh?"

"Well, I hope you agree that you have interesting perks to this job."

"Oh, now that's true," she agreed and then whispered in River's ear, "I get to spend a lot of personal time with the boss."

River laughed, "We both know who the real boss is."

"That's true ... just so you always remember," and she gave him that look of genuine happiness.

Suddenly, they were interrupted by a crowd of well-wishers. It seemed almost everyone from the business was there and in good spirits. They had worked hard all summer. The tension from ensuring all the details of running tours and keeping the tourists happy was finally gone from their faces.

"Another successful summer," River sighed contentedly. "Hope next summer goes as well." He was always planning ahead.

It would have been a perfect day, but then Jack Kelley walked into the group. He was one of the fishermen who had been with the young man severely mauled by The Big One. The bystanders hung on every word as he now recounted the experience. The festive mood changed. Soon several more people started sharing their own versions and sightings of the infamous bear.

"That bear would have to travel at lightning speed to be in all the places where people say they saw him," River pointed out. "I wonder how he can be in 10 places at once." He was surprised that no one saw the irony in it.

People seemed to believe The Big One possessed a powerful ability to travel great distances in a short period of time. They didn't think about it in a logical way. The bear was making the townsfolk uneasy. Very uneasy.

*I wonder what makes The Big One tick*, River thought to himself. *I've been hearing stories of bear problems off and on for the last 30 years, but never has one bear caused so much havoc. How is it he is still alive and coming closer and closer to town? It just makes sense that someone would have shot him by now.*

Then he teased the crowd. "If the papers didn't say they caught and exterminated the bear who slew Timothy Treadwell and his girlfriend, you would all be saying it was The Big One who did that, too."

"Do you think it could have been him?" questioned one naïve and nervous young woman.

River rolled his eyes and shook his head.

"No, they found the contents of the people in the bear's stomach after they shot him."

"Gross," she said and most people laughed at her reaction.

"River!" Sharon said. "Don't be so graphic. That's gross."

Everyone laughed. They were familiar with River's detailed story-telling, as well as the stark reality of Bush living, but most were relieved to have the tension diffused that had built from discussing The Big One. Several had secretly wondered the same thing, *Was this bear still alive, and where would he strike next?*

"What causes a good bear to go bad like that?" Linda Melville asked. Linda was new to Talkeetna. She had only lived there for a few months and the stories of The Big One caused her to wonder if she had made the right decision. "Becoming bear bait does not sound like a good way to die."

"What does sound like a good way to die?" her husband David asked, chuckling.

"Oh, I just want to go to sleep and not wake up," she ignored his taunting. "But not until I'm 100 years old. And I still want to know what makes a good bear go bad."

"Describe a 'good' bear," someone said.

Several people snickered.

Linda sighed. "I can see I'm not going to get a serious answer from this crowd." Everyone laughed again. Linda was good-natured and didn't mind the teasing, but she still wondered what caused a grizzly to behave as if it were stalking humans.

River was wondering the same thing. Something was bothering him about this whole bear obsession. There seemed to be something about the mode of operation of The Big One that was missing from the equation, and it was probably amazingly simple. Thinking back to his early days of hunting and trapping, he recalled the many lonely hours spent walking the traplines. He had tried to "get into the heads" of the animals he hunted and think like them, learn their habits and figure them out. Then he could successfully trap them. He had developed his own technique for trapping, and it had paid off.

He used those same thought-pattern skills in business, to figure out the tourists and the tour guides. He learned how to observe their habits and get into their heads so he could understand what interested and excited them. He used this knowledge to create the right products that would attract them to his tours. He amused himself by remembering he had used the same type of skills to win over his bride.

*So what is the nature of The Big One,* he considered. *What makes him tick? What are his habits? I need to figure him out so I can track and kill him before he becomes a dangerous man-eater. Can't afford any vicious bears eating tourists or anyone else, for that matter.*

Sharon glanced at her husband, and noticed the deep lines of concern that etched his forehead. She had learned to recognize the looks, gestures and twitches that indicated certain anxieties. She thought about what she had heard from many residents, how River was important to this community. She was beginning to understand how responsible he felt for them because they relied on him.

Walking over, she softly asked, "Are you worried about the bear?"

"No, just wondering what makes him tick, is all."

"What difference does it make?" she asked but already knew the answer. She didn't want to admit it, but she was the one totally frightened. She didn't fall in love with this man, leave all that was familiar to her, and come to the other side of the world, to be eaten by a bear.

"Are you thinking of tracking him?"

When he didn't reply right away, she knew the answer.

"May not have a choice," he answered, trying to be as gentle as possible in order not to frighten her more. "It's about time for the bears to hibernate, and I sure don't want him showing up next summer, making more trouble. You know, Sharon, a few years ago, there was another bear causing trouble in areas where I took fishermen, so I had to avoid those spots and find other places to fish. I sure don't want to avoid our excursion areas next summer because of a dangerous bear."

"Could that really happen?" Sharon was suddenly concerned about the possibility of the bear interrupting their river tours.

Suddenly, a local resident by the name of Chet Bastian, who obviously had too much to drink, interrupted the conversation and changed the subject to an even more controversial topic – the environment. Over the years, Chet had determined it was his responsibility to stop the growth of business in Talkeetna. He constantly wrote letters and sent emails to people insisting that Mahay's Riverboat Service was more concerned about making a profit than keeping the village in its unspoiled state.

Most locals suspected that Chet only pretended to be concerned about the environment in order to hide his seething envy of River's success. He often made it known that he didn't like the fact that almost everyone in town had worked for River at one time or another.

"Hey River. What makesh shu an expert on everything, including bears?"

Sharon held her breath, while some people moved forward and others stepped back, each expecting a confrontation.

"I'm not, Chet," River answered.

Sharon breathed a sigh of relief and smiled at her hero, but her reprieve was short lived as Chet continued in his attempt to bait River.

"Really? If that's true, how did you go from a one-boat fishing guide to taking over the whole village?"

The comment confirmed two things. Chet was not only very envious of River's success, but also very drunk.

"The hard way," River answered quietly, keeping his cool and refusing to allow Chet to hook him. "One satisfied customer after another." Then he thought, *if you're not going to do it with all you've got, why bother?*

Sharon was startled by the depth of contempt that was revealed by Chet's comments, and proud of River for not physically fighting back. She also knew he wasn't kidding about "the hard way." River had explained to her that *The Mahay Way* was always a tried and true way, and had always paid off in the long run. But in her opinion, *the hard way* meant difficulty and danger, especially for her husband.

The marketing part of the business assigned to her had to do with attending conventions and meetings with travel agencies that sent thousands of tourists to Mahay's Riverboat Service every summer. She was glad Chet Bastian wasn't aware of her involvement in promoting the company's growth. She avoided a verbal battle with him in front of the wedding guests. Besides, she was the new kid on the block and needed to lie low.

*Who invited him, anyway,* she thought. Sharon was put out with Chet and his constant efforts to discredit her husband and diminish their river business. This wasn't the first time he made derogatory remarks about River. Chet would really be upset if he knew that Mahay's had a new trip planned for next summer. Sharon had high hopes it would attract even more tourists. It was exciting that the little family business had grown to 40 employees and seven boats in 30 years. To Sharon, Chet was so full of what was right for him, he couldn't see what was good for everyone in the community. Sharon had heard that Chet said she was nothing more than a busybody who spoke first and thought later.

She thought about how River loved to share his little bit of paradise with anyone who wanted to see it, and the tours attracted people who loved nature, and wanted to experience it from a safe distance. A lot of his own time, energy and money had been spent to ensure the area stayed pristine.

Sharon was the director of marketing and in spite of troublemakers like Chet Bastian and Big Bear (her reference to The Big One), she was having a lot of fun breaking into her new job. It was exciting and challenging to come up with new angles to attract tourists to take a look at the wilderness through River's eyes and perspective.

While River had spent a lifetime figuring out animals and people, Sharon had spent her career as a child protective caseworker, trying to figure out why some people mentally and physically hurt children. Both Sharon and River had learned a lot about what motivated people to make choices.

Finally, River responded to Chet Bastian, while the crowd of anxious listeners held their breath, thinking a fight would most likely ensue. "Seriously, Chet, I never dreamt I would be making a living on the river, or that I would be doing what I'm doing now. I just wanted to carve out a living for myself, have my family close by, and see if the American dream was alive and well, or even possible. It is, and I think we've all been blessed."

Chet's face turned red and he blurted out, "Oh, really? If you just wanted to carve out a living here, why do you have to keep attracting more and more people by doing such crazy, lame-brained, life-threatening things like you did in Devils Canyon? Can't you slow down before you destroy our little village?"

An uncomfortable hush fell over the crowd as they waited for River's response. He answered with a sigh and spoke softly, but firmly.

"Chet, I'm not sure exactly what you want me to say at this point, but I believe that you and I can be on the same team, because we both love Alaska. Why don't we save this discussion for a more appropriate time?"

Chet glanced around the room and realized no one was going to take his side.

"Okay, but don't think this is over," he said grudgingly. "You have a responsibility to this town and I'm not taking it as lightly as you seem to be."

River considered this comment. *Chet meant well but he really called that one wrong.* Responsibility for this town is why he did about 99.9 per cent of everything. He loved Talkeetna and was grateful for every gift he had received from the sweat of his brow. He even felt a responsibility for Chet and knew he had to walk away from this one. *Pick your battles,* he thought.

"Okay, Chet. Let's enjoy this day and talk later."

Everyone sighed with relief, and returned to the wedding celebration. Finally, it was time to throw rice at the bride and groom.

Soon after, Sharon and River drove home. Both had loved the festivities and sharing experiences with family and friends, but it was good to finally find the time to be alone.

# Chapter Four
# Working the North Slope

"Between Jack Kelley's comments about Big Bear and a drunken Chet Bastian's jealous remarks about you, I thought the wedding was doomed," Sharon said. "I thought Israel and Noah were going to punch him. It's a good thing Judah wasn't there. I'll bet if a fight had broken out, they would have all jumped in."

"You're probably right," said River. "The boys are pretty tired of all his remarks, but Chet usually means well and is pretty harmless most of the time. It's good to have a few watchdogs around. I don't want Talkeetna to become an over-populated town. You know, there was a time when Chet and I were pretty good fishing buddies. Since he retired, though, he's become a bit of a bully, spending a great deal of time complaining rather than finding a solution."

"Complaining is one thing, but picking a fight during a wedding ceremony is something else."

"Yeah, I'm glad it didn't turn into a fight. That's not the way to win him over," he said laughing. "And I'm pretty proud of *My Three Sons*. Remember the popular television sitcom staring Fred MacMurray that aired in the 1960s and 70s?"

"How do you know about an old TV show?" Sharon asked. "When did you ever watch television?"

"I used modern conveniences before living in the Bush."

"I'm impressed. I suppose it would not be good to have your three sons, labeled with biblical names, beating up an old, retired man."

"You're right about that, but Israel wasn't named after a biblical character." River's oldest son, Israel, looked a great deal like his dad and when he laughed you couldn't tell the two apart. His middle son, Judah, was away at college in Michigan, but the youngest, Noah, still lived in town and had also attended the wedding.

"I actually named Israel after Daniel Boone's first son."

Sharon burst out laughing. "Really? That's so typical of you. I can't believe I didn't know that. So, where did Judah and Noah come from? More sons of Daniel Boone?"

"Why Sharon," he said. "I thought you knew your Bible?"

They laughed. "Okay. But I thought I knew everything about you. You snuck that one in on me. What other tidbits of information are you hiding? Please tell me that you've got a pot of gold hidden away somewhere."

River laughed and answered, "I wish ... but no, what you've seen is all there is."

"Oh well. One can hope," Sharon said. "But I do like what I see. Now that you aren't chopping trees and wrestling bears, are you going to change shape and get all flabby?"

"I hope not, but changing shape is a definite possibility. You know I never wanted anything except to live simply and do what I enjoy, like good ol' Daniel Boone."

"I don't think Daniel ever had a business as large as yours," she said. "Did you ever kill bears like they say he did, with your bare hands?" She enjoyed the play on words.

"No, fortunately I never had the opportunity, at least not with my bare hands. I just used a gun."

"Yeah, but you made your own bullets, and I'm beginning to see that *The Mahay Way* is the extremely hard way. Like the way you earned money to buy your first boat by working on the North Slope. I wonder if Chet Bastian is aware of how hard you worked to get where you are."

"You are right about that, and I don't recall seeing him on the North Slope freezing to death. Do you know it gets 60-below zero up there?"

"Whoa. How is it possible to survive temperatures like that?"

"It was difficult, but we thawed out in little mobile units that traveled around with us. Actually, the most dangerous part was working nonstop for several weeks, which caused the men to go a little crazy."

"Uh oh. I knew it. You stayed too long."

They laughed and Sharon asked, "Did you ever see any polar bears?"

"A few. And because we weren't allowed to have guns, we were all pretty worried about running into one of them."

"I just got chills. That's crazy. Why couldn't you have guns?"

"Because the Alaska Department of Fish and Game didn't want us killing ourselves or each other. It got pretty depressing out there. I guess they also didn't want us slaughtering any bears."

"But they didn't mind if men were stalked and slaughtered *by* bears?"

"I'm sure they minded, but hoped we would stay out of each other's way. There was only one man killed by a polar bear while I was there."

Sharon got chilled again, not sure if she wanted to hear the rest of the story. She didn't ask any more questions about this bear because she knew that polar bears stalked humans.

River thought about the tragic polar bear experience and felt it would be better not to give Sharon all the details of the terrible event. He remembered it like yesterday.

The cooks would prepare breakfast for everyone around 4 a.m. The camp was pretty quiet at that time. One morning, one of the cooks walked to the kitchen by way of the washroom. The bear had been waiting there for him. Probably had watched all of them going from one mobile unit to another, and observed their habits for days.

*The bear got in their heads to see what made them tick.*

It doesn't take much for a hungry polar bear to figure out its prey's behavior patterns. It could have chosen any one of them, but this man had been the first one to go to work that day. The polar bear surprised and killed him and dragged him off to eat. The camp employees tried to distract the bear and retrieve the body, but the bear fought back.

The bosses in Prudhoe Bay called the Alaska Department of Fish and Game. After a couple of hours, they showed up in a helicopter. They finally shot the bear, but by the time it was all over, the bear had eaten most of the guy. It wasn't a pretty sight. Fortunately, Sharon didn't ask for details.

"I hope Big Bear isn't a polar bear wannabe," she said. "Could he be half polar bear?"

River laughed and said, "I don't think that's possible this far south."

"Good. But I heard some of the men talking earlier about how The Big One seems to be stalking people, which isn't like a grizzly bear."

"That's true, grizzlies don't generally stalk humans and I don't believe The Big One is stalking anyone, either. I think it's just a matter of being in the wrong place at the wrong time," River said.

"I hope you're right."

"You know I'm always right."

"Oh pleeeaaaase," Sharon moaned.

River laughed and said, "Did you know that because of hardships that can be encountered on the North Slope, it is considered seductive?"

"Seductive? Where did you come up with that word?"

"I read it in an advertisement. Thought you would like it. Do you think it would help advertising if we called our tours and fishing trips seductive?"

Sharon laughed. "I don't think so. No one would believe it anyway. But since the North Slope is supposed to be seductive, perhaps we should go there someday."

"Maybe. But only in the summer," River replied. He wasn't in a hurry to repeat the experience of the freezing weather. "You've ruined me. I like to be comfortable now."

"Good," Sharon said. "I like it when we are both comfortable."

"Are you trying to seduce me?" River asked, hoping.

"Maybe."

"Good. Hold that thought just a little longer. I'll drive faster."

His thoughts were lured back to the extreme experiences from living on the North Slope. "You know you would love the beauty of the Slope. It's a huge, unexplored, rugged mountain range. It encompasses about 89,000 square miles of arctic territory at the very top of Alaska. There is an actual slope in the land and that's why they call it the North Slope."

"Okay, okay. You sound like a geography book. Just tell me how you made money living out in the middle of a frozen world with polar bears stalking you."

"It does sound crazy, doesn't it? But there is a lot of oil that lies in the region from Canada to the Bering Sea."

Before the pipeline was built, exploration crews were sent north of the Brooks Range. River was part of those crews and spent three winters there and one on the Beaufort Sea. His job had been to drill through the ice pack, down to the ocean floor, and set off charges.

This was called seismic drilling. A series of holes had to be drilled about an eighth to a quarter-mile apart in a line. The line ran anywhere from 40 to 100 miles, and a sensor cable was laid on both sides. These cables had to be laid parallel with the line.

He continued, "There were guys who were responsible for attaching little listening devices, called jugs, which were placed in the snow. They called the men juggies."

"Were you a juggie?" Sharon asked, hoping to tease him.

"No, because there wasn't enough money in it."

"Why is that? Because it wasn't dangerous?"

"No, all jobs out there are dangerous. Being a juggie didn't take as much skill. My job had been to drill a hole and place dynamite in it."

"I guess if you were attacked by a polar bear, it would be a good thing to have a stick of dynamite to throw at him." Sharon laughed at the image of River chasing a polar bear with a lit stick of dynamite.

"I thought about that more than once," he admitted.

Every job on the North Slope held a certain element of danger. His job had been to drill a hole between 75- to 100-feet down, and load the hole with a pound of dynamite for every foot drilled. A shooter would later come along and detonate the charge. The explosion sent a shock wave down into the earth, and the crew would listen to the sounds, which would pinpoint fault lines in the earth's crust, because that's where the oil is.

"Besides being dangerous, it would seem to me that it must have been pretty hard work," Sharon said.

"You're right. Between the work, the weather, the loneliness and being completely exhausted every day, it was a brutal way to make a living."

Every day they had had to move the entire camp, which consisted of tracked modular units. There had been three or four D7 Caterpillars, or Cats in camp that pulled the units. Five or six modular units pulled by one D7 followed along in what they referred to as the *Cat-train*. One modular unit had been a dining hall. Another was a washroom, and others had been sleeping quarters. Six to eight men would sleep in each unit, and there were around 30 guys in a camp. River's camp had five seismic drills, called Mayhew 1000s. They were powerful drills that weighed 21 tons and were capable of drilling holes a thousand feet deep. Each drill had a crew, which consisted of a driller and helper.

He described the modular units to Sharon who said, "Oh, I get it. Little trailers traveling on the ice, like a little boy's train set. Sounds like a man's paradise: Huge toys and elements of danger. What could be better?"

They laughed and she asked, "Why haven't I seen any pictures of this?"

"I don't have many and had forgotten that I have a Polaroid shot of the camp. Remind me to find it, when we get home. It's interesting to look at."

River began thinking of the North Slope as if he had been there yesterday. There were times when he was colder, tired and more lonely than he had ever imagined. Every day, the crew moved the camp 10 to 15 miles, but a line might have to be up to 200-miles long. A surveyor crew would flag the place where the holes needed to be drilled. He thought Sharon would enjoy hearing how they got around.

"We rode around in Nodwells," he told Sharon.

"What's a Nodwell?"

"Every man dreams of owning a Nodwell. It's the ultimate vehicle," River laughed. "They were big tractors that moved slowly across the tundra."

Nodwells had been invented in the 1950s specifically for getting through mud and other potentially hazardous terrain. They traveled at two mph.

"Didn't they tear up the land?" she asked.

"Not in the winter. If the work had been done in the summer, it would have definitely damaged the environment, and that's why we had to work in the dead of winter."

"Sounds like getting all that equipment out in the middle of nowhere, plus all the man hours couldn't have been very profitable," said Sharon.

"I'm sure it cost a lot of up-front money to pull it off, but you can be certain it was extremely profitable for everyone, along with the added benefit that it didn't hurt the environment. Using the seismic data collected from the jugs, they could scientifically find the oil reserves without drilling wells. Wells were costly and didn't always produce oil. At the time, seismic drilling was a win-win for everyone."

Sharon interrupted, "So, how did you get the necessary fuel to run all those machines?"

"You ask great questions. That was difficult, too. Doing anything in Alaska took a lot of effort, manpower and time. Nothing was easy."

"So it was *The Mahay Way*! No wonder you did it," Sharon said.

They both laughed. She was right.

River recalled how they had received fuel by air, and had to find a lake to build an airstrip on the ice, because it wasn't feasible to land a plane on the uneven tundra. Since the ice was usually eight to 12-feet thick, it could handle the weight of a plane landing and taking off.

Huge four-engine turboprops, called Electras, had enormous fuel bladders that were used to haul fuel. The Cats pulled the wagons that contained the big fuel tanks. The Electras landed on a man-made runway, pumped the fuel into the tanks, and the Cats brought the tanks back to camp.

River told Sharon, "One time my group didn't go out because the drilling rig broke. I stayed in camp. My boss called over the radio and said a plane was coming in for our fuel drop, but had disappeared. They never reestablished radio contact. We eventually saw a large column of black smoke rising in the sky in the direction of the lake.

"We had a Bell Jet Ranger in camp. Remember I told you I had done a lot of flying in a 206 helicopter? Well, that's how. So we hopped in it and went to see what happened."

River remembered how the Electra had thousands of gallons of fuel on board. By the size of the smoke plume billowing up into the sky, everyone figured the crew was dead.

He continued, "We arrived expecting to find three bodies, but looked down at the other end of the landing strip and saw three guys walking away from the flames. We were thrilled and landed the chopper to pick them up. The only injury was a broken finger."

Aboard the helicopter, the crew told River what had happened. After flying through Anaktuvuk Pass in the Brooks Range, they dropped down to land, heavy with fuel. They chose not to take advantage of a headwind and tried to land downwind, which proved to be a big mistake.

The runway had been long enough for a safe landing, but the plane weighed too much for them to stop in time. There was a hill at the end of the runway, and when they realized they were going to hit it, they turned sideways to avoid a head-on collision and knocked the landing gear out.

River said, "The problem was from one little fire that they saw forming on a wing. In no time at all, the whole plane became engulfed in flames. They jumped out of the cockpit window."

"It's amazing they weren't killed," said Sharon.

"That's for sure. Someone looked out for all of us that day."

The first time River went to work on the Slope, he started out as a helper. Having been raised on a farm, he was confident he could quickly learn how to use the drilling equipment. They wanted him back for the next year, and he had agreed to return to work, but only if they would train him as a driller. They agreed and he went to work in the drill camp. That gave him more money.

"I used the cash I made there to get started in the river business."

"So that's where it came from," said Sharon, finally understanding the rest of the story. "That's the last piece of the puzzle about how you got started, but are you sure there isn't a pot of gold somewhere?"

"Nope. Sorry. I got the seed money to buy the boats from getting paid to work on the Slope."

He recalled there had been enough money to buy the boats and other equipment to get the business going. It took about four years before he was able to make a profit, and River had to keep pumping money into his riverboat business. For several winters, he worked on the North Slope for Western Geophysical.

He said, "You know, they eventually asked me to work in Saudi Arabia, and promised me armed guards carrying .50-caliber machine guns to protect me from the renegade Arabs. I said no thanks. Besides I had enough money by then."

"But that could have been your Alamo."

"That's true. Poor Davy Crockett. Unlike him, I wasn't interested in being a dead hero. I haven't thought about the Slope for years."

"How could you ever forget it?" Sharon asked. "I'm surprised you don't have nightmares."

They laughed.

Speaking of nightmares, River remembered another bad experience on the Slope. It had involved the Rolligon driver. The Rolligon was a big machine with huge wheels that were filled with around 10 pounds of air pressure and used to haul fuel.

Interestingly, a guy from California invented the Rolligon. He had been on a fishing trip in Alaska, and came up with the idea after watching Eskimos remove a heavy wooden boat out of the freezing water over several inflated airtight sealskins. He went home and developed the first low-pressure, off-road tire.

River's crew had a helicopter in camp because sometimes they would need to fly to and from the rigs. Since they could only go two miles an hour on the ground, and had to cover 10 to 20 miles each day, they sometimes would leave the rigs out in the field and ride the chopper back to camp at day's end.

An ex-Vietnam pilot flew the chopper and liked to play around and show off by doing dangerous maneuvers called 'roller coasters.' He had just dropped off River at the camp and immediately loaded the party boss, the Rolligon driver, and a couple other guys. No one ever heard from the chopper again, although it was found later. The pilot had flown it into the side of a hill. With only 30 guys in camp, to lose four like that was a pretty hard blow.

He welcomed the interruption of sad memories when Sharon said, "So, obviously you were able to make more money working out there than you could make trapping furs or prospecting, right?"

"Yeah, quite a bit more. You do the math. I made 10 dollars an hour, worked 14- to 16-hour days, sometimes more, seven days a week and had to go for six weeks at a time. That was a lot of money back then and there was a lot about the job I liked."

"Really?" Sharon asked, surprised. "Let me guess. You liked the hard work, right?"

River laughed, "Yes, I did like the physical labor. Other men had to spend time in a gym lifting weights, but I got in shape from the work I did on the Slope."

"I think just breathing out there would be exercise."

"That's true. It was. But I liked having the skill and being precise."

He remembered how being away from home and family for six weeks at a time was difficult. He lived and breathed his Slope job. He saw it drop to 72-below zero with no wind chill. If it was 60 below or colder, they got a weather day. They didn't get many of them, but did have some days off for whiteouts. Because no one could see anything, and there was nothing anybody could do about it, waiting it out had been the only option.

River remembered one particular whiteout condition. It was the end of the day, and he was driving his drilling rig back to camp. The windows had iced up and visibility was non-existent. He had the door cracked a little, trying to find his way back to camp. Although it had a yellow beacon on top, the office appeared to be 10 miles away. He heard a weird noise and stopped, unaware he was only three feet from the building. He had almost run into the main office trailer. He couldn't tell he was that close, but the coworkers who were in the building could. They had heard the machine coming and said, "He's gonna ram us!" They were ready to dive out of the building.

About that time, Sharon and River pulled into the driveway of their home 10 miles outside of town, off the main road that ran into Talkeetna. They had running water, electricity and indoor plumbing, which was a major upgrade from the house and cabins River lived in previously.

One thing had not changed. River could sense something wasn't right. Danger hung in the air, cold and bristly like the year's first frost. He decided not to mention this gut feeling to Sharon, and planned to work as soon as possible on his bullet loads for grizzlies.

He had reservations about killing The Big One. It was an amazing animal to have survived this long. But then again, it was just another bear. But something had to be done, and soon. Little did he realize it would be sooner than even he anticipated.

# Chapter Five
## Loading for the Kill

Immediately after turning onto their street, Sharon and River observed several neighbors, carrying guns and talking excitedly. Chained dogs barked wildly. One of their neighbors informed them that The Big One had been spotted in the neighborhood.

"Guess that's why he didn't show up at the wedding today. He was here," Sharon said, her voice shaking.

River cast a quick glance at Sharon. She was white as a ghost. What he didn't know was that she also felt weak in the knees, and even a bit nauseated.

"They don't know it was him," River tried to reassure her. "You know how everyone is over-reacting, and if someone now spots a 60-pound bear cub, they swear it's The Big One."

River decided it was time to put an end to The Big One drama.

They pulled in the driveway and Sharon pointed at the garage door as big tears began to roll down her cheeks. River looked in the direction she was pointing and saw paw prints on the door, as if the bear had been trying to push it in. He must have been trying to reach the freshly killed moose hanging in River's garage, but was interrupted before achieving his goal. Fortunately, the moose was still hanging in the garage. River had placed the moose head outside before going to the wedding. The head was missing along with one of Sharon's bird feeders.

"I really hate this, River," Sharon said, finally breaking down in tears. "I don't want to live here, scared all the time."

"I know, but these prints look like this particular bear was about 400 pounds. It couldn't have been The Big One."

"Are you sure? Because if you're not sure, I want to go to the airport tonight."

River laughed, still hoping to calm her down. "I'm sure these prints are not from a bear weighing over a thousand pounds." *The door wouldn't still be there,* he thought.

That night, Sharon eventually fell asleep in River's arms, but only after she made sure he kept his gun near the bed. She didn't wake up when he quietly left the bedroom in the early-morning hours. Of course, it was still dark, but darkness was normal this time of year in their area. He slept fitfully because of what he was about to do—prepare a special load for killing The Big One.

River was sure the recent bear visitor was not The Big One, but something had to be done before fear caused people to go crazy. He could see a massacre of bears coming. He knew that these events could set off a chain reaction that wouldn't be good for anyone.

He considered how Sharon had wanted to see his first cabin in the wilderness and they had planned to go the next day. She had completed all the detailed arrangements for their day together, loaded the backpacks with their lunches and made sure everything at the office was taken care of so River could leave for the day. It even seemed she had somehow arranged for the weather to comply, for it was unusually warm and wasn't raining.

River wondered if she would still want to go, and he needed to be personally reassured they would be safe. As usual, he would be ready for any emergency, even surprise sightings or bear attacks.

He quietly opened the front door, took a quick glance around, searching for any movement, and headed to the garage with his .45 Long Colt in hand. His workshop was there, along with the tools for making his own bullets. Most people just headed over to Wal-Mart to buy a box of bullets, but not River Mahay.

Ask him why, and he'd tell you, "I'm not going to shoot my rifle or revolver in the field until I first know how the bullets will perform. You fire a gun to save your life, whether for food or basic survival. I want to know that my shot will do just that." So he made his own ammunition, and smiled at what Sharon might say; *The Mahay Way*. River believed that if something was worth doing, it was worth doing well, and the tried-and-true methods, which were practiced by trial and error, had saved his life many times.

Until the events of the previous evening, he hadn't realized just how much tension The Big One was causing the people in the area. And not until he was safely in the workshop, with doors closed, did he feel his muscles relax. It was unusual for him to be this edgy. Maybe it was because he was happy now, and wanted to make sure some bear did not disturb his new life. Things were working out well and he wanted to keep it that way.

As River began setting up his loading equipment for his .300 Winchester Magnum, he glanced down at the bench and noticed his old kit for the .45 Long Colt that he had first used in his cabin days. He started to reflect on the beginning of his relationship with the .45, which had started with the friendship of a very dear and trusted man, Peter Stanley. Peter had lived in a cabin a short distance up the ridge and was River's nearest neighbor.

Peter was well educated and successful, as well as athletic, having wrestled for Harvard. He was also a talented musician and had played his guitar and banjo in the same coffee shops in Boston where Peter, Paul and Mary had played. In the late '60s to early '70s, Peter had been one of the most successful investors in the country.

River and Peter immediately became good friends and still maintained contact, although Peter and his family now lived in Virginia.

The handgun was a gift to River for helping Peter build his cabin. Peter was in fantastic physical shape and loved the hard work of splitting and moving logs as much as River. Peter, his wife, Ginny, and small son Christopher had moved to Alaska. They later had two more sons, George and Jimmy. Like River, they had wanted to escape the softening and maddening effects of modern-day life.

River and Peter had a lot in common, except that Peter was well established in the Lower 48 business world. He could go back home to all the comforts American society had to offer. But he chose to stay for a few years. The toll for such a choice was sweat and blood, but the reward was the formation of a life-long friendship.

River admired the many qualities he witnessed in the couple. They could have easily quit and no one would have faulted them for it. Not just anyone could last in the Alaska wilderness. It wasn't just the weather, animals, and lack of creature comforts. It was the loneliness that caused neighbors to rely heavily upon each other, and the constant potential for danger made them willing to help without hesitation. The Stanleys remained in Talkeetna for three and a half years and then returned to Virginia, forever changed, and better for the experience. From time to time, their sons returned to visit the cabin and sometimes worked at Mahay's Riverboat Service during the summer seasons.

River was always grateful for the gift of the .45 Long Colt, and still carries it on his hip to this day. This type of handgun was originally developed as a black-powder pistol and was used to fight in the Indian wars. The bullets are not very powerful by today's standards. Most .45 Colt pistols can't handle modern-day loads and blow apart when used.

Samuel Colt invented the firearm that bore his name, and he purportedly came up with the idea of a revolving pistol while working on a ship where he had signed on as a sailor, bound for India. During his lifetime, in the 19th century, it was said, "God made all men,

Samuel Colt made them equal." It would stand to reason that River Mahay would be attracted to a gun made by such a man.

William Batterman Ruger, founder and chairman of the company that manufactured the .45 Colt, was born in New York. He obviously had a passion for guns, and R. L. Wilson, a firearms historian who wrote Ruger's biography, described him as follows: "Ruger was a true firearms genius who mastered the disciplines of inventing, designing, engineering, manufacturing, and marketing better than anyone since Samuel Colt." River also had a lot in common with Mr. Ruger, and appreciated quality, could recognize it, and was willing to pay the price of time, effort, and money to keep his guns in proper working condition.

Since he had to make his own loads, River bought a classic Lee Loader Kit, because the correct reloading equipment was essential for accurate reloading, and the more potent loads could be safely fashioned. Peter often sat in River's cabin with him at night making experimental loads. They would then proceed to test the loads for killing power.

It seemed dangerous to them that the recommended way to crimp a bullet in place was to tap it with a hammer. Fortunately, they performed the procedure without mishap.

One night, after assembling a few of the experimental loads, they took their pistols outside the cabin to shoot the bullets into a log. After firing, they planned to split open the log to see how deeply the bullets had penetrated and how they expanded. They followed this process of trial and error many times. Believing this particular time to be just another normal procedure, they were caught off guard at what happened next.

They set up a birch stump about 20 feet away and Peter prepared to fire first. Immediately after he fired, he dropped his pistol, grabbed his forehead and screamed, "I've been shot!"

Both of them believed the gun had blown up with pieces of metal hitting Peter in the head or eyes. Running to him, River was finally able to pull Peter's hand away to examine the extent of the wound. He was surprised to find no blood or entrance wound, only a small red swelling.

When Peter realized there was no deep wound or blood, they both burst out laughing. The bullet had ricocheted off the log and hit him in the forehead, obviously proving to them that this was not a potent load. They decided it was time to return to the cabin and have a home brew to celebrate.

The memory caused River to laugh almost as hard now as he and Peter had when it happened. He suddenly missed his old friend, and made a mental note to visit Peter when he journeyed back east.

In the meantime, before he and Sharon left for New York, he

needed to collect and clean all the 12-gauge shotguns used by his guides and ready them for next season. The company provided these shotguns as a means of bear protection and deterrent. The cleaning process involved disassembling each shotgun and cleaning every part, using a toothbrush and solvent. A dirty gun could jam or malfunction, leaving the guide with a useless weapon in a possibly desperate situation. This had never happened to anyone working for him, and River wanted to make sure it never did.

River had learned about guns on the farm. When he was 13 years old, he bought his first gun from money he earned digging potatoes. His father paid him 25 cents a bushel. With this money he bought a 20-gauge Mossberg shotgun, which was great for squirrels and birds in upstate New York. He learned at an early age that a clean gun meant a successful hunt.

He was involved in 4-H clubs that taught leadership, citizenship, and life skills. Once, through the 4-H development programs, he had to exhibit some type of skill for a public-speaking requirement. He chose to demonstrate how to properly clean a gun. What he learned then was never forgotten.

Leaning back in his chair, River swept the bench with his eyes and again stopped on the Lee Loader Kit. It was a basic, entry-level kit and was the first thing he bought when he arrived in Alaska. Next, he spotted an almost empty box of bullets. These were the last of 200-grain hollow points used to kill his first bear and moose. His handloads served him well in the early years, but River was much better at making loads now.

Pulling out the load journal, with all his recorded data, he read the bullet weight, the number of grains of powder used and the primer type. A comment was always scribbled off to the side, indicating the performance of the load under the categories of target, porcupine, or bear. Different powders, bullet weights and primers and their resulting combinations were carefully documented. If the combination wasn't correct, the gun could blow up in his hand.

River knew about loads that were beyond maximum. He had recently put too much powder in a cartridge for the bullet weight, and the rifle could not handle the chamber pressure. The primer had blown out the back of the cartridge. The bullet did exit the barrel, but jammed the action, making the gun inoperable. He knew only too well that in a hunting situation, with a bear coming at him, such a mishap would likely result in serious injury or death.

Over the last couple of years, he'd spent lots of time cleaning his guns and reloading cartridges while talking on the phone to his bride-to-be in New York. Now Sharon was here, sharing his life, sleeping peacefully, trusting that he would always keep her safe.

Making loads for grizzlies was something that River had worked hard for years to perfect, and he had already killed two grizzlies using this precision load, so he had a lot of confidence in the formula. The load he was working on now would be the most important he would ever make.

This was the fall season, so he could hunt and shoot The Big One legally. Since he only killed for food, he usually did not hunt grizzly. Because they were primarily carnivorous, their meat tasted bad. The black bears consumed vegetation such as berries. Their flavor was better. But he didn't want to eat The Big One; he only wanted to protect his world. In situations such as this, that meant kill or be killed.

River was suddenly startled out of his thoughts when Sharon surprised him as she entered the workshop, all smiles and looking fresh.

"Hey you," she called. "Why aren't you still in bed?"

"Just working on some loads. You look all happy and rested."

"Everything is great," she replied. "I'm sorry I freaked on you last night. I think I was just too tired. Can we still go on the picnic?"

"Sure. If you'd like."

"I think it would be fun. I don't want to live in fear, and we'll be leaving for New York in a few days. I'm anxious to see this wilderness cabin that I've heard so much about. I also want to get some pictures of it for our new advertising campaigns."

"You're the best," River said out of admiration and love for this woman he married. "Are you sure you're not already a sourdough?"

"Don't push your luck," Sharon answered softly. "Come back to bed and cuddle with me a while, until it's time to go."

"Twist my arm," River answered. "Why don't we have a picnic here, and go to the cabin tomorrow?"

Laughing, they went back inside, grateful for a few lighthearted moments without fear. For now, life was pleasant and they would enjoy it while they could. They would need these lighthearted times, deserved them actually, to prepare for what awaited them at the cabin.

# Chapter Six
## Living with a Legend

Sharon made the decision to continue with their plans to visit the wilderness cabin. To River, this showed tremendous courage. It seemed New York was responsible for turning out more than one brave individual who commandeered a pioneer spirit. Sharon was from that special breed of survivors that adapted well to most circumstances.

Although she possessed a deep-seated concern about The Big One, she was determined he wasn't going to keep her from enjoying her new life. Besides, she had complete confidence in her husband's ability to protect them. She also knew he would not hesitate to track that bear alone. She couldn't do much to help, but maybe with her around, he wouldn't take unnecessary steps or chances. He was always everyone's hero.

She thought that even though he was a real-life hero, she didn't want him to get hurt on her watch. Besides, it was always more fun to hear about the stories that had already taken place than to be in the middle of them as they were happening.

Pondering her former life, she concluded it would probably seem a little boring to these sourdough mountain people, but she had loved it. She adored her job, apartment, friends, family, her whole life in general. She couldn't figure out what she had ever done to deserve possibly being eaten by a bear, or how she had gotten into this mess.

She laughed and gave thanks to her mom, Darlene, for making sure she grew up with a sense of humor, remembering the great comment her mother had made recently, just before she had left Talkeetna after a short visit this past summer.

"That's what started this whole mess in the first place!" her mother said as they headed toward the store where she and Sharon had first met River Mahay.

Everyone burst out laughing. It was a perfect comment to relieve the tension that had been building over the last few months from trying to figure out how to live in Alaska and New York at the same time. It wasn't working very well, and the separations were hard on mother and daughter, who were used to seeing each other practically every day.

"The mess" to which reference had been made was the marriage of Sharon to River. A mess, thought Darlene, happens when a city girl from the East Coast falls in love with an Alaska sourdough who happened to be a legend to boot.

It did not make Darlene feel any better that River was legendary or that he had made many rescues off three dangerous rivers. She wanted to think of Sharon in a little cottage with a white picket fence, without bears or dangerous river rapids on the horizon.

It had not been a whirlwind courtship, and there should have been plenty of time for everyone to get used to the idea. Both Sharon and River took their time trying to examine the possibilities and solve the problems that would arise from this love triangle between them and Alaska.

But Sharon was Darlene's only daughter. Her husband, Sharon's dad, had passed away a few years prior to the "unfortunate" once-in-a-lifetime Alaska cruise. Unfortunate, because now Sharon was married to this mountain man, and lived on the other side of the world.

Darlene had always wanted to visit Alaska, but her husband had never had any desire to do so. Later, Darlene had taken care of her mother, putting the visit further into the future. Gram eventually went on to her great reward, and Darlene convinced Sharon the time had come to visit the Last Frontier. Arrangements were made for a cruise through the Inside Passage, with an added land package. They boarded their ship-of-fools, unaware of the transformation that was about to take place when Sharon and River met on one of the riverboat excursions.

Thousands of people take trips each summer with Mahay's Riverboat Service, and to Darlene's dismay, this man and her daughter connected as if they were long-lost soul mates.

Darlene understood being in love, for she had deeply loved her husband. She still missed her daughter, however, and worried about the dangers she might face from living in the wilderness.

It didn't take much for River to notice Sharon that first day, for she had an outgoing, easy personality, and practically glowed with beauty inside and out. Her perfect New York accent reminded him of the place where he had been born. He could not help becoming immediately infatuated with everything about her.

Sharon was five-feet, four-inches tall, with a slender build. She was only 42 years old, with long blond hair, and big blue eyes that twinkled when she laughed or when she realized he was teasing her, which happened often, for he loved to tease. So did she. They could both dish it out and take it.

"A perfect match," sighed a disappointed Darlene.

River was amazed Sharon had never been married and was even more astonished at his good fortune in finding her, and then being able to convince her to marry him. It was entertaining and exciting for him to discover what made her tick and figure out what her hopes and dreams were. The two main things they had in common were a strong will and a sense of fair play. They would need them to get through the hard times that were coming soon.

Much to River's joy, Sharon was also full of integrity, compassion and intelligence. She had graduated from Valparaiso University in Indiana, just like her big brother, Paul Heim. Both were athletic, and good at running, keeping slim and trim. River was also a runner.

Sharon graduated with a major in social work and a minor in marketing. Social work fit her caring personality and investigative nature, especially for child protection. She easily talked to children, who immediately opened up and trusted her. This profession allowed her to practice natural skills of empathy, a characteristic that came easily and that River particularly admired. It was what made her good at marketing.

Sharon loved people and the only part of her job in New York that she did not find enjoyable was testifying in court, as she found the drama of courtroom battles to be difficult on the little ones she protected. She much more enjoyed gathering facts, and being able to communicate well made the work easier. Sometimes the stories told to her by the people she interviewed didn't match, but her skill or second nature was always to question everything, and she was able to read through the hype and get to the truth. This always paid off in the long run.

Sharon found people fascinating and she figured them out quickly. This was another characteristic she and River shared. Her formal education perfectly prepared her for the marriage to River along with her new career.

She loved soft rock from the '70s, had a pioneer spirit, and for some reason, which River could hardly fathom, she loved him. What could be better?

The trip to Alaska by mother and daughter had been booked through a travel agent in New York. Before the cruise, they were to go on the train from Anchorage to Fairbanks. It stopped in Talkeetna, and included a riverboat trip.

River and Sharon had to be brought together by divine intervention, for neither one was actively seeking a companion. Both were living comfortable lives, fully committed and busy. Sharon says River didn't notice her until she was in the small gift shop in the office.

The cruise part of the trip, through Alaska's Inside Passage, took place last. Sharon and her mother were on the ship on September 11, 2001, and no one could convince Darlene this was not an omen or sign of more bad things to come down the road. They were stuck on the ship for a few days, which in her opinion was a grand finale to their less-than-memorable moments.

Before they left New York for the cruise, Sharon's good friend, Angela, had predicted that perhaps Sharon was going to meet someone special. Sharon scoffed at the idea and didn't give it another thought until later. Looking back on the message, Darlene decided it had been a warning, and should have been heeded.

Before the trip, Sharon was convinced her mother might meet some nice elderly gentleman, but never expected that she would be the one to end up in a long-distance relationship, and subsequent marriage to a riverboat man from Alaska.

"Really, who would have thought it could happen?" Darlene said out loud as she and Sharon laughed, giving her mother a bear hug.

Many men had asked for an opportunity to contact her over the years, and some never called. She did not expect this one to be any different, but before she even returned to New York, he made contact.

Darlene should have seen the handwriting on the wall, but she liked River a lot and thought it had been very exciting for Sharon. It wasn't supposed to last. Something went terribly wrong. The passing fancy was now her son-in-law.

*How does anyone live with a legend, anyway,* she thought.

In trying to figure him out, she watched the videotapes of his amazing Devils Canyon run. They were impressive and she enjoyed telling her friends and family about his exploits. She once watched the video on the Discovery Channel before meeting him, but didn't know anything about him or his world then. She was concerned for Sharon's safety because of the daredevil in him. Now she was intimately aware and torn between loving him and watching how happy her daughter was, while feeling a void with Sharon gone. Life certainly had a way of twisting things around.

She wished her husband was still alive, knowing he would have loved River, and been proud of his daughter. She felt that Sharon had courage and the nerve to follow her heart, as well as being a wonderful person, caring, fun to talk to, and thoughtful. It seemed to Darlene that Sharon must have been waiting all her life for just the right man, and she had found him. River Mahay.

"Just why couldn't he live closer to New York," she sighed. But what was just *was*. So she dealt with it, because that's what people did who loved one another. Sometimes, like in this case, things were not easy, but her faith had her convinced it was always worth it.

*Besides, I can still talk to her every day,* Darlene reasoned. *But what about those bears?*

Sharon knew her mother would really go over the edge if she heard about The Big One, so she wasn't going to mention it.

She told River, "I feel like I'm in high school, sneaking around and telling my mom half-truths."

"Did you do that in high school?" he asked.

"No, but I had friends who did."

"Right." And they both laughed.

"Aren't families wonderful?" Sharon concluded. "Hey, I wonder if bears have families?"

"Sure they do, but I doubt if they tell half-truths to their mothers."

"Yeah," Sharon said. "You're probably right. They just lie outright. Seriously, I wonder what goes on in a bear's head."

"Survival, mostly, regarding where their next meal is coming from."

"I just don't want to be that meal," Sharon said. "But, you know, they were here first."

"So I've heard," said River.

Then Sharon studied the contemplative look on her husband's brow and wondered what he was going to do about The Big One. She knew he was up to something because River was a doer.

## Chapter Seven
# True Grit

There is a constant stress when practicing independent survival in Alaska. Men and women who are called to it live for the rewards, which are treasures that are storehoused deep within the heart and soul.

There are many, however, who cannot survive because they find the work too hard or just can't stand the loneliness. Each person has only so much time to live, and few if any truly know when their time will come. Some will say that because of this, it is important not to be bothered by the inconsequential. Each individual has a personal definition of what's important. There are those who figure it out, because they devote their lives to the things they love, and cherish the people most important to them.

Sharon and River were two such people.

They traveled upriver toward River's first cabin in the wilderness, with a full picnic basket, some water, a first-aid kit, and of course, a rifle with River's hand-loaded grizzly cartridges. He hoped they wouldn't see one, or at least not The Big One, while Sharon was with him.

He had that feeling again that they were being watched and even followed, but maybe it was just his nerves, which were a little on edge because of all the commotion in town. People were frenzied over this bear, and River knew it was coming down to a battle he would have to fight on his own.

Perhaps returning to the old cabin sparked this melancholy. He had forgotten how much he missed the cabin. Memories flooded his mind. It was a long time ago, but it felt like yesterday.

On July 17, 1972, River had staked out an area to homestead, about 10 river miles from Talkeetna. It was on a ridge overlooking the Susitna River, with a majestic view of Mount McKinley and the entire Alaska Range.

There he built his new home, a 14-by 16-foot log cabin, using only hand tools and what the forest had to offer. Sixty-five logs were used, 19-to 21-feet long, with 126 poles for the sod roof. The floor was dirt. He had brought the chimney and a homemade stove with him. He spent the dark, cold, winters living off the land. It was a tough life, but one he had prepared for by growing up on a farm.

His access was the river, which meandered through the valley floor, and also the railroad that was a quarter mile below the ridge. The train stopped for people who stood in the middle of the track and waved a white handkerchief tied on the end of a stick. To acknowledge a slowdown and pickup, the engineer would toot his horn twice. Back then, the cost was two dollars per person. It was called a flag-stop train. To stop for anyone was the way of the railroad and the Alaska frontier. Life and death in Alaska teetered on a fine balance between people who lived far apart from each other. All were connected in some finite way and survival depended upon honoring this fact.

River used a chain saw for the first time to cut planks for a table and two chairs. He split logs using an axe. To make a door, he had to find logs with true grain in order for them to split evenly, leaving a flat surface. He also split logs for a sleeping loft. The surface of the loft ended up being uneven, but no matter, it worked. A mountain man couldn't ask for more.

*If you are tired enough, you can sleep on most anything,* he'd say.

He was glad to have learned many valuable skills on the farm such as the ability to work hard, grow crops, tend animals, hunt, trap, chop wood, pitch hay, build fires, and a thousand other simple skills which prepared him for survival in the Bush. Especially his skill of trapping, because animal pelts brought money to buy food staples, supplies and tools, and the meat provided sustenance. Nothing was ever wasted.

The dark winters were long, lonely, and cold, more frigid than anything back east. Sometimes the weather dropped to 60 below. Not everyone could last out the winters, but River did, because that's what legends do.

*Where better to test and defy the laws of nature, and feel passion to be alive,* he often contemplated.

There were chaotic weather conditions, gale-force winds, scattered fog layers, freezing temperatures and wild river rapids. The air currents changed continuously over the mountains, causing harsh conditions such as whiteouts that covered miles and miles of remote areas. This all added up to danger for most individuals, but to River Mahay, it was stimulating and fulfilling, even spiritual. For some odd reason, he was content and happy in this environment.

Weather conditions could change from calm to major storms and challenge even the best woodsmen. Alaska was proving to be the perfect place for him to test, push, and discover himself. He found the spectacular views of snowcapped mountains, blue glaciers, cascading waterfalls, prehistoric-like wildlife and unpredictable weather to be breathtaking, and the many near-death experiences, exhilarating.

River had discovered when he was very young that he had unusual talents for hunting and trapping. He was a natural for living off the land, as well as the river, and could read signs most people never noticed. These talents crossed over into the piloting boats on dangerous rivers. Today, many say that his boat piloting is like that of no one else. He doesn't drive the boat; he wears it.

Alaska woodsmen truly belong to a breed of their own, and for some strange reason, unbeknownst to many, especially from the Lower 48, they appreciate the sensitive and sometimes unforgiving living conditions in which they find themselves. They are okay with extreme situations where everything fails, especially modern conveniences, such as batteries, supplies and engines. This is a regular occurrence.

Living in the Bush had strengthened River physically, mentally, emotionally and spiritually, thereby opening his mind to many of life's secrets and mysteries. Some things he knew were true at a gut level—such as how to live with courage, instead of being fearful. River had always trusted his Maker, to whom he gave the credit for his will, fortitude and strength to survive. He learned how to live with gratitude and passion, instead of the doldrums or taking life for granted, by seeing things he could never see anywhere else in the world and understanding things only the ancient Eskimo and American Indians understood. They understood because they lived it. This wasn't something a man could learn from a book, it had to be experienced, and if he survived, it hopefully became ingrained. River worked on fine-tuning his automatic reactions because he didn't have to waste time thinking about how to respond to danger, in the face of it.

Something happened to a man who learned to live as a partner with nature, rather than trying to fight or change it. Something deep and hard to describe, but something that answered the unanswerable questions such as *Who is Man*, and *What is Man's Purpose?* Living in the wilderness, and facing death on a daily basis provided River with the ability to enjoy the journey of learning and acting out that purpose.

That's why in the beginning he refused to buy or use chain saws or man-made materials while building most of his cabins. He wanted to feel the oneness, the connection between man and God, with every chop of the axe. This not only brought him closer to recognizing his own weaknesses and strengths, but also caused a oneness with the eternal world.

Man living in society searches incessantly for balance between the workforce, family, and health. The woodsman, however, works within the laws of nature while defying death. He finds that balance and, rather than feeling he must conquer it, he joins with it, becoming one.

River could hold his own against all that Alaska could throw at him, and toss she did, to see if he deserved to share daily in the beauty she offered. From the bears, wolverines, and other dangerous wildlife, and the long, dark, cold winters, to the occasional two-footed varmints, extreme temperatures, and loneliness, Alaska was a jealous mistress and required all the strength a man could muster from the depths of his being to survive. Her rewards were breathtaking; her penalties for mistakes or weaknesses were often fatal.

That's why Alaska woodsmen are considered the best in the world. Merely surviving in Alaska developed a true grit in a man, building character along with muscle. A man living like this couldn't help but learn to listen and understand life on a higher plane, hopefully causing an internal gentleness to form for his stewardship over God's world, along with the building of physical strength. For some, the hardships were too much and they left, returning to an easier life.

*Couldn't cut the mustard,* River thought. *Many try, but only a few make it. I've seen a lot of wonderful people come and go. They find the elements and dangers too hard or can't come to terms with the loneliness. They love the quiet at first, but the stillness and solitude can be the hardest thing to overcome.*

There are more men than women living in Alaska, and for some, living alone in the Bush creates a look of wildness, sometimes mistaken for rudeness. This characteristic might result from a lack of social opportunities. There is a longstanding joke describing this phenomenon of the Alaska mountain man's characteristics, along with a woman who might hope to find herself a husband there. It goes, *the odds are good that you will find a husband in Alaska, but the goods are odd.*

Living with nature doesn't always necessitate practicing what society might refer to as good manners. There are times in the Bush when Lower 48 good manners might get a man killed, such as thinking bears are cute and cuddly.

The trick is to know the difference. Some men figured out how to live with nature without fighting it, while still remembering how to apply the social graces. Rare individuals, like River Mahay, recognized that strength did not have to exist exclusive of kindness and manners. They could go hand in hand.

On another note, he had seen a lot of tragedy on the river and in the mountains, but instead of giving in to grief by allowing himself to become cynical, he learned to appreciate that there was a greater good or cause for all things. Hard work, gratitude, a willingness to help others, and an appreciation for his Maker along with His greater plan, all added up to the development of his character and nature.

It's not just the death-defying stunts on the river, nor the many exciting near-death adventures that are legendary, although some of them could give Indiana Jones or Crocodile Dundee a run for their money. The man himself is legendary, from deep down inside. *The only way for man and beast to live side-by-side in the wilderness is to be forever wary of each other. Take only what you need to survive, and never kill for pleasure,* is River's life slogan.

He saw animals that killed for pleasure, and met men in and out of the wilderness who did not honor life. These were the savage beasts of the world. He wasn't one of them, although one had to be prepared to kill, or not survive. River always carried a gun, and he stayed prepared.

In the early days, there were only a couple of ways for traveling when the train wasn't running. In the summer he used the river, and in the winter, he used dogsleds. The dogs were a way of survival, but hauling dog food up the hill to the cabin wasn't easy. It was best done in the summer by the river, and then packed up the hill to the cabin on foot. This work kept him muscular and didn't give him time to develop love handles or a beer belly sported by his friends back east.

River learned the history of this land, and, like Lewis and Clark, was a great storyteller. He loved to tell the story of the Talkeetna people who were called "the mountain people." Originally, the area was inhabited by a group of people called the Dena'ina. From 1924 to 1926, influenza wiped out about 95 percent of the tribe. Locals referred to them as the "Apache of the North." The Russians had tried to trade with them, but were cruelly abusive, enslaving the young people through rape and murder. The natives fought back by refusing to trade with them.

The Russians sent an exploratory expedition up the Susitna River, but it never returned. Everyone figured the natives had killed them, and the Russians would not go back. This fear kept other people out for a long time. Not until the discovery of gold around 1896 that explorers, traders, and prospectors went back. There were about 800 natives who lived at the place now called Susitna Station. They made skin rafts by bending saplings and wrapping moose hide on the outside to create a bowl-shaped raft for floating the river. Fish were a huge part of their lives, and the river was their highway.

River speculated on all this history while keeping an eye on the river. "A penny for your thoughts," Sharon shouted over the engine of the traveling riverboat.

"I was just thinking about the local Indians and the cabin. Thank you for wanting to see it. I didn't realize how much I've missed it."

"There is so much of you in that cabin," Sharon explained. "I just want to get a feel for what you accomplished, plus the pictures will be good for marketing." She poked him in the side and they both laughed.

"You are really good for me, do you know that?" he said.

"Yes, I know. But go ahead and tell me more."

"Because you make me laugh and see things from a different perspective. I'm fascinated by the way you look at the world."

"Why? Because it isn't *The Mahay Way?*" Sharon asked.

"I guess. But it's more about the level of compassion you have for everything you see and everyone you meet."

"You just haven't seen my bad side yet. But don't worry, it's coming."

"Now that worries me! Do I get a warning?"

"Of course. I imagine you will be the one who brings it out!"

"Remind me never to do that."

River guided the boat to shore, and Sharon jumped off and tied the rope to a tree. River followed with the backpacks, his rifle and camera. They put on their packs and started up his so-called well-marked trail, which was nothing more than a bear path. Both wore hip waders while hiking through fierce-looking devil's club; plants despised by hikers because their sharp spines slice through a pair of jeans and into the skin.

After traveling a short distance uphill, Sharon asked, "I thought you said this was a well-marked trail."

"It is. We're on it." He didn't want to tell her it was a well-used bear trail. *Better to stay away from the "b" word*, he thought.

"I thought you said it was an easy hike."

"It is. We're almost there."

"It feels like we are going straight up."

"You're out of shape."

"I beg your pardon," Sharon said.

"I mean, I like your shape."

"That's better." Sharon was becoming winded. "Can you slow down a little?"

"Okay. Let's rest for a moment." River noticed a spot where a bear had been lying down and felt the area to see how long since the bear had been there. It was still very warm.

Sharon glanced around. They were deep in the woods, about a half-mile from the river. "You packed in everything to the cabin?"

"Yes. If you wanted something, you packed it in; groceries, supplies, dog food, kitchen sink, towels, pumps, stove, bathtub, books, and games. There was only one way to get it there, on your back."

"I would have had second thoughts about marrying you if you still lived here."

"You're safe. I don't want to live out here again, but it was home for five years."

"Were you insane back then?"

"Some suggested I was, because I loved it. Ready to get going?"

"Lead on, Kemo Sabe."

They stopped talking and concentrated on the climb. The devil's club was brutal but did not puncture their thick rubber waders. The trail was barely visible, but River seemed confident in knowing exactly where he was going. As they got closer, he moved faster, excited to see the cabin again.

Sharon was determined not to lag behind. She followed at a fast clip and tried not to think about the many dangers that surrounded them, especially the bears.

River was constantly watching for signs. He carried his rifle in two hands, ready to use at a moment's notice if necessary.

They reached the top of the ridge without incident, and there it was. The cabin. It looked smaller than Sharon had imagined.

"I didn't know you built two cabins up here."

"The smaller one was built for a visitor's cabin and then it became my workshop, plus I stored firewood there. I didn't build it as well as the first one."

They walked over to the cabin door that was ajar.

"Stay back," River said gently. "Let me check out everything first."

"Hello, hello," he called out, while pushing open the door with the rifle. Sharon held her breath and jokingly looked around for a tree to climb. Since The Big One was said to be over 12-feet tall, she would have to climb fast and high to get away from him.

"All clear," he called out, and went through the door.

Sharon ran in behind him. "Don't leave me out here alone," she scolded, and looking over his shoulder, said, "Wow. What a mess."

River looked sad. Bears had broken into the cabin and trashed everything. There was nothing in the cabin that had not been chewed on. Sharon picked a book off the floor called *Instant Sourdough*.

"This looks interesting. Shall we take it home?"

"Yeah. I think the author signed it."

"So did the bear," Sharon pointed out. It had slobber on it and teeth indentations. "Guess the bear didn't like what the author wrote about him."

They laughed, but it was sad that the bears had destroyed everything in the cabin.

"Will the cell phone work out here?" Sharon nervously inquired.

"Yeah, but probably not inside the cabin."

There was an indentation on the couch where the bear had been lying down. Sharon felt shivers run up her spine, and felt like Goldilocks in the story of *The Three Bears*. This made her laugh and distracted her from the chilling thoughts running through her head.

"How did you get water up here?" she asked.

"We had to haul the water from the spring at the base of the hill. We carried it up in five-gallon jugs. Eventually, we got a submersible pump and generator. Would start it up and fill a 55-gallon drum placed in the loft. Then gravity would feed the water to the sinks and gray-water drainage outside. But all this took time and money. We didn't have all those luxuries at first."

Sharon laughed, shaking her head. "I didn't need to know all the details. Like I know what a gray-water drainage thing is. What about bathing?"

"Now, baths were a very serious thing. Once a week, maybe."

"Gross," Sharon wrinkled her nose, and they both laughed.

"This stove must weigh a ton," Sharon said, pointing to an old cookstove. "Don't tell me you carried it up here, too?"

"I did. Only one way to get things here. Nothing was easy. Everything done out here is a major chore. Peter and I made this table with his chain saw. First time I ever used this tool. Felt like I was cheating, but that thing was pretty handy. I felled a tree and made the legs."

Sharon studied the room, trying to get a feel for the man who lived here. Was he the same man she married? He had not done all this alone. His first wife, Kristine, had come out here with him. River didn't speak much about his first marriage, and Sharon respected his privacy. Either the breakup had been too painful, or he just wanted to keep the past in the past. Sharon knew they must have been deeply in love to do all this together. Also, what an amazing woman to have followed her man out into the Bush, and agreed to live like this. *Perhaps she didn't follow him, but he followed her,* she thought.

"You want to straighten up things a little?" Sharon suggested.

"No, not now. I need to come back when we have more time and fix the door, as well as do other repairs. The roof still seems pretty good."

"Nice windows. All the panes are broken out."

"As the cabin settled, the panes broke about two years ago."

River recalled a funny story about that window. His brother-in-law and wife, John and Katie, had visited River at his cabin and stayed for a while, helping him build a second cabin. They also brought their newborn baby with them.

He told Sharon, "I traveled to New York in 1975 or 1976 to visit my folks, since I hadn't seen them in four years. While I was in New York, a bear had gone through a window and ate a whole bottle of aspirin, bit through every can we had, and tore off everything on the walls. It was a horrible mess."

"Worse than this?" Sharon asked.

"Yes, because we had more stuff to destroy. We spent the next day cleaning up. Since we had no place for guests to stay, they brought a pup tent, but didn't want to be far from the cabin, for fear of bears."

"Gee, imagine that," Sharon said, "being afraid of bears."

"Really," River agreed. "What were they thinking? The first night, the tent was set up about six feet from this door. We had a hide-a-bed and the foot of the bed was under the window, which was the same one the bear had broken and come through. I kept a gun over that window. There was a plastic garbage barrel in which I used to make homebrew, and it was sitting between the cabin door and the pup tent.

"It was early July, so it didn't get dark. They kept a rifle inside their tent. About midnight we heard a strange clunking noise. Looking out, we discovered a bear had his head in the barrel and his bottom was pushing into the tent. John couldn't turn the long rifle around to shoot him, because there wasn't enough room. They quickly scrambled out the back of the tent. Their movement startled the bear and it ran away.

"We watched the back end of the bear disappear over the side of the hill. I figured he was gone and wouldn't be returning.

"Everyone went back to bed, and it wasn't 10 minutes later that we heard that clunking noise again. That bear was standing in front of this window, here, looking at us, and the window was obliterated with the black fur of the bear's chest."

"Oh, my gosh. I would have died right there." Sharon shivered while looking at the window. "What did you do?"

"Well, I was trying to figure out what to do. I remembered seeing a movie once, where John Wayne shot someone through window glass, and I wondered if it would work in this instance."

"John Wayne? Oh, no. I bet you did it."

"Yep. I loaded one of my potent handgun rounds and shot through the glass window. The glass shattered and the bear fell, but got back up. I stuck the .45 Colt through the broken window glass and shot again. He didn't get up."

"How scary. What did John's wife do? I bet she was petrified."

"She sure was. Two months later, she packed it all back home and divorced him."

"Over the bear?"

"Don't know for sure, but stranger things have happened."

Sharon stood there looking out the window. "I wish you hadn't told me about that. I really can't think of anything more frightening than seeing a bear in that window."

River was sorry he had told the story and tried to distract her from any more bear thoughts. "You know, I built that other cabin for them to stay in. Was sorry it didn't work out."

"I guess you can call that your guest cottage. Does it have windows in it too?"

"No. I never put windows in the other cabins. Makes it harder to heat, and just another place for critters to get in."

"That makes sense. How did you insulate them?" Sharon asked while she examined the material between the planks, glad for the change of subject.

"That was pretty ingenious, if I do say so myself," River laughed as Sharon rolled her eyes. "I took the moss and crammed it between the logs, a process called chinking. When done properly, the chinking keeps out the drafts, so the cabin can be easily heated. It obviously held well, because it is still here 30 years later."

"Amazing. What about the heat? Where did that come from?"

"Well, as you can see, the cabin isn't very large; the inside dimensions are only 14 by 16 feet. I heated with a Sears wood-burning stove bought for the small fortune of 47 dollars. It had a surface area on top, which was also used for cooking. In later years, I modernized by adding a propane cooking stove."

Sharon couldn't believe all the simple things in life that she and most people took for granted, such as heat, water, and electricity. Just turn a knob or flip a switch, and voilà, you had simple conveniences. She liked it that way.

"In the winter, I had to melt snow to get water for dishes and for cleaning. The drinking water always came out of the spring, and I was pretty fortunate, because there was a wonderful spring close to the cabin, with awesome drinking water. It never froze. It was a lot of work hauling it up the hill, but by then I had running water." River paused.

"How did you have running water?" Sharon bit.

"I would run down the hill and run back up with it."

She rolled her eyes, while shaking her head, laughing. "You nut. Guess that was the epitome of running water."

"Is epitome a brand name?" he teased.

"You know what I mean," Sharon said and punched him in the arm.

"Okay. Okay. I had a big tub, and in winter I took a bucket outside, scooped up the snow and dumped it into the tub. It melted and we had all the water we needed. I also had an Alaska Bush washing machine, which looked like a glorified toilet plunger. It churned the clothes, and then we hung them out in the freezing cold. They froze solid, but when they thawed out, we had clean clothes."

"Impressive. I feel grateful for running water," Sharon said.

"Me, too," River admitted. "I like our luxuries."

"Excuse me. They are not luxuries. They are necessities."

"It's all relative, isn't it?"

"No. This is very important to our future together ... to me, they are necessities."

"Got it." he laughed as he walked through the door to check out the other building that Sharon called the guest cottage. Every log in both buildings was etched into the memories of his muscles. Chopping and moving, trying to quickly build the shelter for protection from the elements and animals, as well as a comfortable home.

His brother-in-law had lived in the guest cottage for about a year. It was a nice workshop and the woodshed was always stocked. Looking around the debris, he found part of an old chain saw. Memories flooded his mind.

He had a flashing thought of Kristine, who was so much a part of this place. He would fell a tree and they dragged it back to the cabin to be put in place. They encouraged each other to keep moving, but she was much smaller than he and after a while, she became too tired and was unable to go on. She sat down on the ground and cried. There were usually berries on the ground where she dropped. Sitting there, crying, she ate the berries. Then after getting her fill, she got back up, picked up her end, and they moved on. She had guts, energy, and a never-give-up attitude that matched his own. But then, for some reason, they gave up. It had been five years since the divorce.

River thought, *relationships are the most important things in life, but it seems for some reason we forget, getting caught up in things that don't matter in the long run. Men don't need as much as they think, to survive in this world.*

Sharon was also thinking about relationships, while examining all the nooks and crannies of the cabin, and wondering about his life with the first Mrs. Mahay. She wondered how they had lived through all this, only to divorce each other later. It seemed they had made it through the rough spots.

*I don't want to live without the amenities of the modern world,* Sharon thought. *I'm glad I came along later, and didn't have to share his wilderness experience. Kris is one amazing lady to have lived out here.*

Both were deep in thought, and did not notice that a shadow had crossed the doorway. The room darkened. Sharon turned, thinking it was River. What she saw was her worst nightmare come true.

A huge grizzly's head weaved back and forth inside the doorway, viewing Sharon as both intruder and prey.

River turned when he heard the deep, guttural growl, the type that makes you turn hollow with fear. What he saw sickened his stomach, yet instinct took over. Every cell in his body snapped to attention as he shouldered his rifle, looking for a clean shot that would drop the bear quickly. His rifle sights revealed nothing but fur. An exposed area on the chest flashed. A possible heart or lung shot was risky at this distance. The bear could still maul them to death before it died. His trigger finger tensed, but did not squeeze.

The bear glared and growled at Sharon. Its teeth snapped in anger as sharply as an igniter on a gas stove. Sharon moved only her eyes toward River, pleading, begging for help. Any movement would trigger a savage attack.

Sharon stood motionless as if flash-frozen in ice. She was in that place of total fear where even the thought of screaming was frozen into inaction. She was helpless, defenseless, and she knew the bear was ready to attack and kill her.

Suddenly, when fear couldn't sink its poison any deeper into his heart, River heard another growl, louder and more ferocious than the first. He glanced to his left. Another grizzly as large as a small car shot out of the brush, its massive frame churning and rippling under layers of muscle and fur.

River raised his rifle, and his finger tensed. He had to make the first shot count, and the closer the bear, the better.

Just as he was about to fire, he quickly raised his head and moved his finger away from the trigger. The bear wasn't attacking him, but angling toward the bear in the doorway.

The charging bear slammed into the other and River felt the ground shake from the impact. The momentum rolled them into a snarling ball, head over tails into the open. In a horrifying cacophony of roars and growls, the battle began. Huge forepaws swung as swiftly as a major league slugger, backing a power that could send a man flying through the air. Thick canine teeth flashed long and yellow. The bear's powerful jaws were strong enough to splinter a moose leg bone as easily as a human bites a toothpick in half. For a few seconds, time stood still.

The bears kicked up dirt and snapped trees as they rolled, bit and swatted each other over the edge of the ridge and down toward the train track and riverboat.

River knew this was their moment to escape. He ran into the cabin where Sharon stood, frozen in fear.

"Sharon, are you okay?"

"Am I dead?" she whispered.

He loved her sense of humor, and was amazed it was still intact. "No, not yet. But, let's get out of here."

"I'm not sure my legs will work."

"Tell them that those bears may come back, and we need to be somewhere else."

"Okay, they've agreed."

Sharon and River grabbed their packs and ran down the trail to Peter Stanley's deserted cabin. It was the only trail to avoid the bears. From there he would find a way back to the boat.

# Chapter Eight
# Running for Life

It was a short distance over to Peter's cabin, which a bear could cover in seconds. Yet River wanted to put as much space between them and the two bears as possible. Now that the immediate danger was over, there was time to reflect on what had actually happened. If he hadn't known better, it seemed the second bear had saved Sharon's life. But that was ridiculous. It was more likely he just had a bone to pick with the other one.

"Do you think one of those bears is The Big One?" Sharon asked, interrupting his concentration.

"Yes I do," he answered.

"Which one?"

"The second one."

"I know this sounds odd, but I have a strange feeling that he saved my life. Is that possible, or do you think it was by accident he showed up in the nick of time?"

"I was just wondering the same thing," River admitted. "Perhaps he wanted us for dinner, and the one in the doorway was messing up his chance. I don't think bears go around caring about saving human lives."

"Yeah, that's what I was thinking … just hoping I might be wrong, and we had met a noble bear."

"That would be nice," River agreed. "But not likely."

At the pace they were walking, they would reach the cabin in a matter of minutes. River noticed the forest had grown and covered up most of the trail between the cabins, as if no one had ever walked there.

Peter's cabin was much larger than his, and circular in shape. They could rest here for a few moments, and then double back to the railroad tracks below, and on to the waiting boat.

He had his cell phone, which was another change from his past Bush life. Originally, he had no way to communicate with people

unless they were within hearing distance. Then, as others came trying to carve out a living, they checked on each other or fired three
shots into the air when they needed assistance.

Eventually, citizen band radios helped people stay in touch and
individuals didn't feel so alone. Later, when cell phones showed
up, they ended up saving lives, because precious time was saved or
conserved in looking for missing or late boats and adventurers. River
chuckled, thinking about the time when Trapper Tom lived out here
and River was his only contact with the world.

"What's so funny?" Sharon asked. She could stand a little bit of
humor at the moment.

"I was just thinking about a guy who lived out here for a short
while. We called him Trapper Tom, but he wasn't a true woodsman.
He was a cab driver from New York City. Anyway, he was out here,
supposedly living his dream, and had selected a Navy Arms rolling
block .45-70 government gun for protection. Not a good idea."

"I can't believe you remember what kind of gun he had," Sharon said.

"Well, sure," River explained. "You could tell if someone was going to be safe by the type of gun he used. His was a single-shot rifle
that was developed in the late 1800s, using a very old black-powder
load, so it took some time to reload. It couldn't shoot far. Up close,
it had substantial knockdown power, but you had better be on target
because you had only one shot. Trapper Tom never had any experience with bears before he moved out here."

"Me neither," Sharon said. "And in my humble opinion, that's not
a bad thing."

"I know and I'm sorry, honey. You know I wouldn't let anything
happen to you."

"I know, but I shudder to think what might have happened if Big
Bear hadn't knocked Demon Eyes into tomorrow. But, go on. Finish
the story."

"Demon Eyes? That's funny. Okay. Trapper Tom quickly discovered he was living in the middle of a highly populated black bear
area. He started seeing them every day and became more and more
concerned. Over the course of a couple of weeks, a bear showed
up in his yard and then investigated the porch. He shot at it, and
believed he wounded it, but the bear ran off into the woods."

"What's funny about that?" Sharon asked, feeling an affinity for the
frightened, would-be bear victim, Trapper Tom. "I can't believe you
are laughing at that poor man. After looking that demon bear in the
eyes, I can see why Trapper Tom was scared. So, what happened to
him? I don't want to know if the bear ate him."

"No, he wasn't hurt. He contacted me by radio around midnight in mid-June, when it was still light. He was really upset and asked me to help find the wounded bear in the woods. He insisted it was a grizzly and threw in, for good measure, maybe even The Big One, just to make sure I would come."

Without even saying so, Sharon knew River had gone to assist Trapper Tom. It was just something he would do without hesitation.

River continued. "Now, understand that Trapper Tom was definitely out of his element, but I wasn't thrilled about the possibility of facing off a wounded bear, especially if it was a large grizzly. When I arrived at his cabin, Trapper Tom showed me where the bear had run into the woods. I was surprised to find a bloody trail."

"He really did shoot the bear?" Sharon was impressed, but wished they were sitting at home in front of the fireplace telling this story, rather than out here in the open, waiting to see if another attack was imminent.

"He shot something, but the tracks weren't big enough to be a large bear. I felt a bit uneasy following a trail that could possibly lead me to a wounded, crazed bear. I went about 25 yards, and found a 40-pound dead black bear, obviously not our Big One. Fortunately, after that, Trapper Tom decided not to spend the winter in the Bush. He left, stopped off in town to embellish the story and no one ever heard from him again."

"Wasn't that fairly risky, going after a wounded bear, especially when you were told, albeit mistakenly, that it was The Big One?" Sharon asked.

"It was something anyone would do," River said. "Going to someone's aid, because an animal is injured. It could be dangerous leaving a wounded animal out there, plus inhumane."

Sharon heard what he said, but didn't believe it was something just anyone would do. It was something River Mahay would do, while thinking it was nothing out of the ordinary.

"*The Mahay Way*," she sighed.

Then she added, "I don't blame him for leaving. I wish we were in a cab in New York. I used to think they were dangerous. Now I'm feeling crazy taxicab drivers are much safer than hanging out here."

River thought it best if he ignored Sharon's comments about wanting to be back in New York, and said, "I didn't blame Trapper Tom, either, for his sake or mine."

He added, "Oh. And another thing. When Trapper Tom left, his story changed dramatically. The black cub had changed into a 600-pound grizzly bear."

"That is funny," Sharon said. "But I have to say, bears look a whole lot bigger when you're looking them in the eye."

"Speaking of looking them in the eye, you did great back there."

"What do you mean? I didn't do anything but freeze, waiting for you to do something to rescue me. I felt like one of those dumb girls in the movies that do nothing but scream, run, and trip."

"You didn't do anything dumb. You were perfect. I figured I had about two seconds to get in a good position to get a hit that would make a difference. The only thing I could see was this huge back end blocking the cabin door. If I shot him there, I figured he would jump forward into you."

"The only thing I could see was his demon eyes. I was actually wondering how you could possibly shoot him without making him jump the rest of the way into the cabin. I couldn't move. I've never seen anything like that in my life. He was just glaring at me with those beady little eyes, dark with death. I can understand that I'm lower on his food chain, but why did he look like he hated me so much?"

"Fear, I guess. He obviously had some unfortunate encounters with humans and is carrying a grudge."

"Maybe Trapper Tom wounded him." They laughed, but River knew that a lot of people didn't know what they were doing and that people caused most human-bear troubles. The bear glaring at Sharon could have been wounded at some time, and now he was one ticked-off monster, truly a demon.

"What about the second bear?" Sharon asked. "I never did get a look at him, thank goodness. I don't think I could have stood seeing two of them in one day."

"He was larger than the one in the doorway."

"You're kidding!"

"Nope. I was trying to get a clean shot when the other one came out of nowhere and charged. It was as if he didn't even see me. He went straight for the one that was staring you down."

"That's a stare I won't soon forget. I hope we don't have another encounter with him. Did you know there were two huge grizzlies out here?"

"No, but it makes sense. It explains how he has been in two places at once."

"I hope there aren't more of them. A whole family of giant grizzly bears. Let's get out of here, now, please."

The shock was beginning to wear off, adrenaline was dissipating and Sharon had had enough. River was also feeling exhausted from the experience. Seeing Sharon so close to danger had taken its toll.

"You know I killed my first bear, right there by that tree?"

"Really? Was it another big grizzly?"

"It was the largest grizzly I had ever seen up to that point in my life, plus I had never before been that close to one."

"What happened?" Sharon asked, grateful to be hearing another story and not living in the nightmare of her own reality of what had just happened and wasn't over yet.

"Peter had gone back east for a visit, and he asked us to periodically check the cabin. We heard something, so I came over to investigate, and discovered a huge bear trying to get into his cabin. It turned on me, and immediately charged, but stopped about 10 yards in front of me. Then it stood up on two legs, which proved fatal to the bear. I was new to Alaska and my nerves were shaking, this being the first time I faced a charging bear. I was shaking badly enough that I was unable to hold the gun steady for a clean shot.

"You know, thinking about what happened that day reminds me of something I read in *Alaska Bear Tales*. I can't believe you still have the book. Can I see it for a minute?"

"Sure," Sharon handed it to him as she realized she was still clutching it with all her might.

"Here it is. Listen to this: *'No doubt many bears have gone to bear heaven because someone misinterpreted his false charge, and there are many men who have been chewed on by bears because they assumed the bear was only bluffing.'*"

No truer words had ever been spoken. But River's motto: *Don't think, just react,* along with the successful survival technique developed for living in the Bush: *It was better to be safe than sorry.* That's what he had done that day, but had forever regretted taking advantage of such a shot.

"I moved quickly to rest my gun against a birch tree. When I pulled the trigger, the bear went down. I couldn't believe it. Just one shot, and she fell down. Talk about being frozen. I just stood there with the rifle still aimed at the dead bear, waiting for her to get up. But she never did."

"How did you know it was a she?" Sharon said.

"That's the part I regret. I stood there for what seemed an eternity, then went back home to get my tools to cut her up. When I got back and started working on her, I heard some movement in a tree behind me. I turned slowly around, walked over to the tree, and was sad to find three cubs up there, watching me. I felt sick to my stomach as the reality of what just happened washed over me. She had only been trying to protect her cubs. They were helplessly watching the whole thing."

"Oh, River, that is so sad. Did you save them?"

"Tried. Was going to take them to the animal preserves. They would have finished raising the three of them, and then all would have been safely released back into the wild."

"What a good idea. I never thought of that."

"Well, I thought of it, but those cubs thought differently. When I reached up to take the first one out of the tree, I saw nothing but teeth and claws. Another little guy was hissing and swinging at me. I tried a couple of times, but they all did that hissing thing. There was nothing I could do, and just said, 'Okay, little guys. Have it your way.'"

"What happened to them?"

"Well, they stayed in the area, getting into people's trash, breaking into cabins, and eventually two of them were killed. Never knew what happened to the third one. Hopefully, he survived. Hated to think I was responsible for their deaths. I always hoped that the remaining one survived."

"Wouldn't it be strange if The Big One was the third cub?"

Hearing Sharon speak those words out loud startled River. He had often wondered what happened to the third cub. He wondered every time he spotted a bear following his boat on the ridge. He had seen a bear when he was doing the Devils Canyon run, but never felt he was in danger, just being watched out of curiosity.

"That would be strange," he answered. "But I venture to say that the third cub is long gone by now, or more likely would be your demon bear instead. I'm sure that cub did not appreciate what I did to his mother."

River scanned the bush surrounding the cabin, looking for any sign of impending danger. He had a gut feeling all was well and they should take this opportunity to head toward the boat.

"Ready to start back?"

"Am I ready?" Sharon replied. "I've never been so ready."

"I'll take that as a yes. Hey, I thought you wanted some pictures."

"Oh yeah. Sorry," Sharon answered. "I forgot all about pictures, but we can improvise and use someone else's photos."

River, carrying his rifle in a ready position, led the way over the ridge and to the train tracks. They would follow the tracks to the riverboat. If the train appeared, heading for Talkeetna, they would flag it down and ride back to town. He would pick up the boat later. He just wanted to get Sharon to safety.

If tourists found out there were two monster grizzlies causing havoc, they would definitely be hesitant to visit. River had that feeling again. Someone was watching. He picked up speed, but suddenly glanced over his shoulder to take a last look at Peter's cabin and the tree where he had tried to save the cubs. There was The Big One, watching him, from behind the tree. The bear made no move toward them.

Then they heard the sound of the train whistle.

"Come on, Sharon," he called, starting to walk faster. "Let's take the train back."

"What about the boat?" she asked, suspicious that he might be trying to dump her and go back to wrestle the bear on his own. She said, "I'm not going without you."

"Don't worry, I'm going back on the train with you. I can pick up the boat later."

Then Sharon knew they were in danger. He would never leave the riverboat unless he suspected there was a chance they would run into the bears again.

# Chapter Nine
## Flag-Stop Train

Sharon and River stood in the middle of the tracks and waved a white shirt at the approaching train. The Alaska Railroad was the only train in the United States that continued to have this flag-stop service and the locals were grateful for the opportunity to catch a ride when needed, especially Sharon and River.

When the train stopped, they jumped on board and good-naturedly withstood all the questions and teasing comments from the conductor and other passengers regarding why they were on foot. Everyone knew River Mahay and his reputation for having many boats on the river highway.

Now that they were safely on the train, they comfortably settled down for the short trip back to town. River reflected on the many times he had relied upon the train for survival. Most people living outside of town counted on the train for supplies, travel, and news from family or friends. There was a time when it had meant everything to him.

The train would come once a month and he would order, whenever possible, about 100 dollars of groceries, which consisted of a five-pound block of cheese, five pounds of bacon, some eggs, and things of that nature. Things he couldn't get off the land.

One particular month he placed an order and waited for the train, but it went right on by and didn't stop. Kris had sat down and cried. He tried to comfort her by pointing out, "Look we're not going to starve. We have everything we need to live. So we'll do just fine."

It was pretty depressing though, because they didn't get many of those wonderful comfort foods. To most people, these foods are staples but in the wilderness, they are luxuries, true comfort foods. Not getting the supplies meant they would have to eat more beans and rice, plus any berries they could pick, along with whatever he could shoot. River had known they would be okay, but it was pretty upsetting.

The following day, when the train came back on its southern route, it stopped. They had just forgotten to drop off the order. The panic had been for nothing. Just another test, and they had passed.

The rhythmic sound of clanking over the tracks along with the gentle swaying motion rocked them into a peaceful drowsiness, while feelings of contentment washed over River and Sharon. It was only about 10 miles to town, and each one was taking advantage of the time to rest and enjoy the ride.

River considered how the land in this area was extremely familiar to him. He had traveled it many times. Reverting to another time and place, he thought of when he trapped and hunted on a daily basis. Trapping was a skill he had learned early in life on the farm, but the wilderness had provided the opportunity to really practice and develop it. The experience and work had been deeply gratifying.

It had been a long time since he had walked those traplines, and compared to the two bears seen today, those animals had been smaller and not particularly dangerous to a careful trapper.

Sharon noticed the worried line in the center of her husband's forehead, and by the way his eyes were glued to the passing landscape, she felt sure he was thinking about their recent experience.

"What are you thinking about?" she asked.

"I was thinking about the time when I lived out there and trapped for survival." He nodded toward the window and out in the Bush.

"Was it awful?"

"No, just pretty intense. I really liked the lifestyle, back then."

"I can't imagine," she sighed, "especially after today. I'm glad to be leaving soon."

"I know. I am too, believe it or not."

"Really?" Sharon was surprised that he wanted to leave Alaska. She thought it would be hard for him to go away, even for just a few months this winter.

"Yeah. It was the right time to come 32 years ago, and it's the right time now to take a break. I've been fortunate."

"I once heard, the harder you work, the luckier you get."

"Hey, I like that. You couldn't help but work hard living in the Bush, and while trapping out on Clear Creek, there were many times when I felt pretty lucky to be alive."

River began thinking about the history of the area. He had known where all the Indian sites and digs were, because he had often hiked the region of Clear Creek. On the other side of the river from where they had been today, he found the pits dug by the Dena'ina Indian people, who were part of the Athabascan nations. The first contact with them was made a little over 100 years ago and only about 75 years before he got there.

A prospecting expedition led by William Dickey around 1896 gave details about these people, and quite a bit was known, because he kept a journal that described an Indian encampment discovered there. Of course, they didn't speak English and no one spoke the Dena'ina tongue, but he had written descriptions of their clothing and the articles used, realizing they were living then as their ancestors had lived several thousand years ago.

Their animal-skin garments were made by hand with primitive tools. They lived in an earthen lean-to, with sod over the top, leaving one side open, where they built a huge fire.

The temperatures in that region could be as low as 60-below zero, so it was obvious these people lived a pretty tough life. They ate primarily caribou and salmon. There were 5,000 who lived in the valley back then, and they were known as The Mountain People. Fish were a huge part of their lives, and the river was their highway.

The pits were holes in the ground, like big refrigerators where the Dena'ina would store dried fish. They dug them close to camp, to protect their food from animals.

River said, "On tomorrow's tour, we'll make a stop at the replica of an Indian encampment, and everyone will be able to have a visual aid for how the people in this area had lived."

Sharon said, "I love how you share your wilderness world with people who would never know about such things."

"Thanks. You know, I built the encampment just for show, but in the same way my other cabins were built. The real ones, out in the Bush, were built because I needed places to stay while working the traplines."

"Your early days in Alaska sound like another world. It's difficult for me to comprehend that the man you describe is the same man sitting here with me now."

"It was another world, very different from our lives today."

"Tell me what you did on a regular, normal day."

River picked up a flier that was on another seat. On the backside, which was blank, he drew an illustration of how he would set up and then walk the traplines, along with the location of each item he was describing.

"See, this is where I established four different lines, away from the cabin, making a big circle, and forming this four-leaf clover pattern. Each line was about five miles, with 15 traps set. The best or most lucrative line was up at Roger's Mountain and an optimal day was when I caught six marten. One marten pelt brought anywhere from 30 to 60 dollars, which was a small fortune back then. I could buy a lot of supplies with that kind of money."

Sharon said, "You worked hard for 30 dollars, and that amount is so easily wasted today. But I never heard of a marten. What kind of an animal is it?"

"Marten are a little smaller than house cats and live in trees. They feed on small birds, shrews, squirrels, eggs, and berries. They hunt all night, and rarely go near the water. A large population can thrive in a small wilderness area because there is so much for them to eat. Since they live primarily in trees, I placed the traps there, and became pretty good at catching them. I sold their skins to a fur buyer, who would in turn sell them to a furrier."

"I know that's predominantly what you trapped, so why haven't I heard of them before?"

"Oh, you've heard of marten, just by a different name. Furs made from marten are referred to as sable." Then River hesitated until the word sank in, and he was never disappointed. All ladies knew sable.

"Sable! Wow. So, where's my sable coat?"

He laughed and said, "I had to eat back then before I could think about decorating a pretty lady."

Sharon looked at him with a pouting expression, and said, "Okay, for now. But you aren't totally off the hook. Continue with your story and attempt to distract me from the picture I have in my mind of me in my beautiful sable coat."

River cleared his throat, pretending to be nervous, and continued to explain about his workdays on the trails.

"The hike back to my cabin was 20 miles, which had to be done in one day, in the early days, because I only had the one cabin."

River sometimes used a three-dog team, and eventually expanded to a five-dog team, but only used the dogs to haul supplies to and from the cabin. The dogs were big and strong, especially the village mongrels. Strays, found wandering around town, were grabbed and put to work by whomever found them first. Once, while heading to the cabin, the five-dog team got quiet and acted skittish. They had come upon a place where a pack of wolves had just crossed. Dogs are fearful of wolves. Wolves have been known to sneak into Talkeetna and kill tethered sled dogs.

River learned early on to listen and watch the behavior of the dogs, because they saw and heard things long before a man could. They had also been helpful in transporting supplies and quickly covered long distances. On the other hand, they were an enormous amount of work. They needed to be trained properly, and obviously needed food. Their provisions had to be packed in along with everything else, and when available, he would boil meat for them. Sometimes they were a little picky, and didn't want to eat what he served, but if they got hungry enough, they would eventually eat.

"Brute, my lead dog, once ran after a moose. He was gone for a whole day and I figured he wasn't coming back. It was during the last night of a bad storm, and as if his running away wasn't bad enough, I got lost, too. Having already laid the trail, I was pretty far out and spent four days hiking through a region of about 100 miles."

"Since there was an early fall storm, the snow had thawed and the rain caused a lot of slush. I got damp late in the day, so I was getting colder by the minute. After hiking for a while, I found a stream and knowing it either went to the Susitna River or Clear Creek, I followed it."

"Why didn't you use a compass to figure out where you were?"

"Good question," River answered. "The immediate problem in this area was that there were heavy metals in the rocks, which prevented the compass from working correctly. To further complicate the situation, because of the storm there was no sun; so between these two conditions, I could not get a good feel for the right direction that I needed to travel. All I was sure of was that I had to get to the river, and once there, I would have my proper bearings.

"I eventually found a big spruce tree and made camp. In order to survive I needed to build a fire, but by that time I was hypothermic. My hands were so numb I couldn't hold a match. Everything I had on was wet. Even my six-pound sleeping bag was so saturated with water that it weighed 30 pounds.

"Gently and carefully, I prepared tinder knowing I had only one chance to start a fire. It had to work the first time."

River paused, allowing the emotion of the situation to affect Sharon's sympathetic nature. If she hadn't been so completely engrossed in his story, she would have noticed how a slight twitch was forming in the corners of his mouth, as he tried not to smile.

"Then what happened?" Sharon leaned forward to hear his answer.

"Not much," River simply stated. "I froze to death."

# Chapter Ten
# Clear Creek Survival

"Very funny!" Sharon exclaimed, and smacked him in the arm. "Why do I listen to you? Now, tell the truth."

"Okay," he laughed, "Sorry, I couldn't resist. Actually, the fire started and thanks to the small, warm blaze, I thawed out, boiled some water to cook dried beans and rice which I always carried with me, and then gratefully ate until satisfied, rested somewhat, and survived another night."

"I guess in some ways, we aren't much different from the animals," Sharon reasoned. "If we get hungry enough, we'll eat anything. But beans and rice without condiments, doesn't sound very appetizing."

"Ah, but," River added, "I also carried condiments or luxuries, if you please. You see, I had a small amount of salt and pepper."

Sharon said, "Salt and pepper ... are luxuries?"

River nodded.

"We sure take a great deal of things for granted in the real world of modern conveniences, don't we?"

"That's right," River agreed. "But in the wilderness, nothing is taken for granted, and when morning came, I was still in trouble, because I continued to be wet and lost. The good news was the fire had provided what I needed to buy some time, as it had thawed out my hands, enabled me to cook some food that filled my belly, and given me some time to rest. I didn't intend to allow the situation to get that bad again."

"If you were still lost, and without shelter," Sharon interrupted, "it seems to me the situation was already bad."

"Well, I knew better than to go as long without the warmth of a fire, I still had some food left, and most importantly, I had stored away some significant information that I had once learned at the Fairview Inn."

"Oh my gosh. I never know when you are telling me the truth or not," Sharon said. "What did the Fairview Inn have to do with being lost in the wilderness? It sounds like you took a survival course there, or more than likely, are pulling my leg again."

"No, I'm serious, and that's a perfect way to describe it," River clarified. "The Fairview Inn was potentially the best local survival course for the smart individual who went there and listened to the stories from the hikers, trappers, prospectors, and locals."

The gentle swaying of the train running along its tracks caused Sharon to comfortably lean back her head, close her eyes and scoot down farther into her seat while she listened intently to River. He quietly explained the details of how he had prepared for the unexpected experience of being lost.

"Once when I was visiting the inn, I heard about an abandoned prospector's cabin, built by a guy who came out of the hills with pockets full of gold. Supposedly, it was just on the other side of the river from where I had been trapping."

"But it was on the other side of the river," Sharon said. "And this was before you had a boat?"

"That's right."

"Then how could you benefit from an abandoned cabin you could not reach?"

"Another good question by my brilliant bride, as well as a point in favor of the Fairview Inn," River explained. "I heard tales that some trappers had strung up a cable from one side of the river to the other, and supposedly it was not far from the prospector's cabin. Since this was about 20 miles from my cabin door, if I could establish a way to cross the river and use the abandoned cabin, it could prove to be quite beneficial and timesaving."

"What if it was just a rumor? Or they lied? Or, even just made it up for a fun story to tell?"

"Then I would have to come up with Plan B."

Sharon laughed, shook her head and looked lovingly at her very own Indiana Jones husband. He always had a Plan B in mind, just in case. She silently realized how grateful she was to be a part of his life as it was now. Those early days sounded very exciting but it was more fun hearing about them than physically living through them.

"How would you even go about locating a cable in hundreds of miles of frozen nothing?"

"Well, that was the tricky part. I had to use a process of elimination. I hiked a trail two miles from my cabin door, went downriver, and then across the peninsula to Clear Creek. This was part of the area that I regularly trapped, and since I had never seen the cable in that area before, I decided to follow the course of the river. If it was truly there, I would eventually run into it."

"That sounds similar to how you were able to make so many successful river rescues," Sharon reminded River. "I guess this way of searching prepared you for finding and rescuing people later?"

"That's right. I followed the river for several miles, and then, sure enough, there was the cable crossing. The river was deep at this point and didn't freeze over in the winter, and the current was dangerously fast. But the cabin I needed was on the other side, and I still had to figure out how to cross using the cable."

"I can't wait to hear how you managed this one," said Sharon, as she settled back in her chair to listen, still grateful she hadn't been with him back then and trying to imagine how he could possibly make it across.

"Well, I needed some type of basket big enough to get supplies over. I brought rollers to attach and slide over the cable, just in case it did exist, so when I found it, I was somewhat prepared."

"Oh my gosh, you think of everything," Sharon exclaimed. "Now you are an engineer."

River laughed. "You really need to know how to perform a lot of different skills in the wilderness. Again, it helped growing up on the farm and having to make do with whatever we could come up with on our own. I knew how to use the items that nature provided to make whatever was needed.

"And, at the moment, what I needed was a platform large enough to carry me and supplies across to the other side. So, I made a sturdy type of wooden basket out of two pieces of wood with smaller sticks lashed between them. I suspended them from two V-shaped pieces of wood, attached to the rollers. The unusual-looking contraption actually worked."

"How could you be sure that it would work?" she asked.

"I wasn't sure it would hold. But, I laid on my back, and went slowly, hand over hand, and moved myself carefully across the river. It held."

"So, it worked for getting the supplies across, too?"

"It did, and finally I was on the other side and went to search for the prospector's cabin. Then sure enough, I found it. The cabin's floor measured about eight by ten feet, and the roof had caved in, but it was usable. I had found my base."

"So the Fairview Inn saved the day."

"It sure did, but it was going to take a great deal of work to restore the cabin. The logs were still up and the main beam was intact. I figured if I put up a new roof, applied sod, and installed a wood-burning stove, I would be able to heat it. I couldn't do it alone, so I got a friend to help."

"Speaking of a friend, I just thought of something," Sharon said. "We are supposed to meet Don Lee tonight at the Fairview Inn for drinks."

"Oh, that's right." River was glad she reminded him. "I'm looking forward to a little rest and relaxation, and it's been a while since we hung out with Don."

"It will be good to see him again. Was it Don who helped you repair the cabin?"

"No, it was Ralph Martin."

"So, now you also had to get Ralph and the building supplies, including a stove, across that cable?"

"Yep, but not all at the same time. We made several trips."

"Thank you, River," Sharon said as she threw her arms around his neck and gave him a passionate kiss.

Pleasantly surprised, River matched her fervor.

Sharon asked, "Don't you want to know why I thanked you?"

"Okay. Why did you thank me, and so creatively?" Whatever he had done, he wanted to do more of it.

"I'm grateful for not being married to you back then."

River burst out laughing and squeezed her tighter. "I don't blame you," he agreed. "Don't blame you one bit. Now that I had the cable basket built and the cabin livable, I was ready to go to work."

"What? You did all that labor, just so you could go to work? The amount of effort it had taken to locate the cable, build the basket, then find the cabin, cross back over the river, hike to the cable with supplies, move everything across the river and rebuild the cabin, was not considered work? What was it then?"

"Preparation."

For the life of her, Sharon couldn't figure out why he had done it all, and told him so. "Why would anyone in their right mind want to do all that preparation?"

"Because I found each step of this process rewarding," River explained. "And it was all done to make sure I could do my job efficiently, plus be safe. It paid off more than once, but particularly the time when Brute ran off and I got lost."

"How long were you lost?" she asked.

"About four days, and by the end of the fourth day, I was still following the stream, but beginning to recognize some landmarks. I determined I was much closer to the prospector's restored cabin than the 15 miles back to mine."

River recalled the feeling back then that survival was becoming risky, because he had been getting low on food and was in dire need of shelter. He had known that time was running out. Spending another night exposed to the elements had not been an option.

"Then, amazingly, I found an old prospector's trail that led me to the river."

"So you were saved."

"Well, not quite. I still had to cross the river, to reach the warmth and safety on the other side."

"But what happened to the cable and basket?"

"They were still there, but a storm had caused an overflow and this time I faced the dilemma of crossing higher river water, with complete fatigue overpowering my body, and hands and arms that refused to move."

Sharon said, "I can't take much more."

"I know the feeling," River agreed.

"Are you making this up?"

"No, it's all true."

"It sounds very complicated and risky."

"I suppose so. Do you want to hear the rest of the story?"

"I don't know. Are you almost safe?"

"Almost." He continued. "So, I cautiously sat in the basket, praying it would hold my weight above the high water. I went hand over hand, carefully and painfully crossing the river."

"Why was it painful?" Sharon asked.

"Because my hands were frozen, I was exhausted, and the temperature was 25 below."

"Oh, is that all?" They both laughed.

"I suppose you were carefully crossing because you didn't want to fall into the river."

"Right. I knew I wouldn't last two minutes in the freezing water. My hands ached from the frostbite, plus they were cracked and bleeding, but I had to keep going the 40 yards to the shelter on the other side of the river."

"Another crisis?"

"No, nothing else went wrong, at least not at this point. The cable and basket held. When I reached dry land on the other side, I fell out of the basket exhausted, but very much alive."

Sharon said, "I'm worn out just hearing about this."

River laughed and continued, "I finally made it back to the refurbished cabin, and made a mental note to visit the Fairview Inn on my next trip to town. I planned to share my appreciation and testimony about the existence of the prospector's trail that led to the river, knowing that this information might someday save someone else's life, too."

"Did something happen later?"

"Of course," and River laughed, while Sharon closed her eyes, threw her head back and said, "Oh no."

"It's going to be okay. In the cabin I kept two kerosene lanterns, because they burned only about four gallons a week. Remember that all supplies had to be packed in and carried across the river, on the cable, so the lighter the weight of the supplies, the easier it was to get them to the cabin. I lit the lanterns and finally began to thaw out."

"I can see why it was important for you to have the use of this cabin," Sharon said.

"Yep. It really paid off that time. Otherwise, I had to find and reach my cabin, some 20 miles away. I probably could have made it, but it would have been risky."

Sharon laid her head on River's shoulder and they both closed their eyes for a moment and silently expressed gratitude for the life they now had, as well as the lessons learned from the past.

River's soft voice broke the comfortable silence as he said, "There is an unwritten law of the Bush, that each time you exit a cabin, you leave all the necessary makings of a new fire beside the stove; tinder, kindling, firewood and matches, because this could make the difference between life or death—your own or that of someone else. If you stay in someone's cabin, it's customary to leave a note thanking the owner for its use. This is the accepted and courteous thing to do."

Sharon said, "I am impressed with how people in the wilderness are willing to share their possessions and help others in need."

"It is one of my favorite characteristics of the people who live here," River agreed.

Sharon pointed out, "Can you imagine pulling up in the driveway in suburbia and letting yourself in to take a shower? Eat a little meal and then be on your way? You'd probably spend the night in jail."

"That's right. Do you want to hear the rest of the story?"

"I'm not sure ... yes, go ahead."

"You'll like this ending. Well, after I thawed out that day, I started the woodstove with the makings of the new fire that I had previously prepared. It felt good to be back in the safety and warmth of a cabin with my hands thawed out. Plus I was fortunate not to have sustained permanent damage."

"I was completely exhausted, however, but grateful to be alive. I soon realized I was more hungry than tired. I didn't have much energy in order to cook anything fancy, so I just placed a can of stewed tomatoes on the wood stove, which would have been perfect, except for one minor detail."

"Uh, oh," Sharon said.

"I forgot to punch a hole in the can."

"Oh no! I know where this is going," she chuckled.

"You are right, because, of course, as soon as they were slightly heated, the can blew up and sent stewed tomatoes everywhere."

They had a good laugh and Sharon said, "Remind me to keep you out of the kitchen." She marveled at how adept he was in the wilderness, while a little clumsy in the kitchen.

"You are such a man," she teased.

"Thanks, I think, but no problem ... the kitchen is all yours. Fortunately, I wasn't physically injured by the attacking tomatoes."

"Isn't it ironic that you avoided all that tragedy out in the wilderness, only to be almost blown up by a can of stewed tomatoes? No one would have believed it."

Laughing more, River said, "I thought the same thing. After the tomato-bomb incident, I rested. I seemed to be better equipped to find food in the wilderness than in my own kitchen. I decided though, it was time to sleep, and it came easily and deep. I didn't wake up until midmorning."

"I'm not surprised. It probably felt wonderful to rest after all you had been through."

"Really. It did. Later, when I woke up, I was stiff and sore from the ordeal, but it was time to get back to work."

"Guess there is no rest for the weary?" Sharon asked.

"No, none, and it was time to forge on."

# Chapter Eleven
# Modern-Day Trapping

Over time, River built several trapper cabins, so at the end of running a trapline, he would end up at a cabin. This made the work much more enjoyable, and the workdays shorter. He would check his traps every five to seven days, to make sure they were still operational, and the sets had fresh bait. Usually, about a third had to be reset each time because an animal had succeeded in pulling off the bait.

Every cabin had been fully equipped, especially with stretcher boards, which were shaped like a small ironing board. A hide would be case skinned, meaning only one cut was made from one hind foot to another, and the hide pulled down to the nose, and removed. It would then be rolled and pulled onto a board as you would pull a sock onto your foot. The purpose is to stretch the hides tight so they would dry and keep their shape. This also prepares and preserves the pelts until they are sold to a fur buyer.

The stretcher boards were handmade because there was no place to buy them. They were sized specifically for a particular animal. Each of the cabins would have two or three stretcher boards, one for marten, one for fox, one for wolf and one for wolverine or otter.

After River described this process to Sharon, she said, "I will never again wonder what people in Alaska do all winter. I don't know how you found time to do everything that needed to be done."

River had learned to do all the chores involved in trapping by listening to other trappers and reading a lot. But his personal best way of learning was still by trial and error, or *The Mahay Way*.

He caught mink, occasionally in the Talkeetna Mountains. Both mink and marten are in the weasel family. Mink are always smaller than marten and a dark brown, almost black color. The darker the color, the more valuable the fur. Mink are excellent swimmers and would travel many miles of waterways searching for food. The marten is more of a nocturnal animal, and except for their tracks, both are seldom seen in the wild.

River explained to Sharon that he used the whole animal when trapping, and nothing was wasted.

"I still hunt for food to this day, but seldom trap anymore, except for business accounts, which is part of your job," he teased. "Whenever I can find bears, I eat them. Black bear is good to eat. It's hard to tell the difference between a bear burger and a hamburger, because about 90 percent of their diet is vegetation. The black bear's average size is only 150 to 300 pounds. The much larger grizzly frequently eats rotten fish and carrion, which often gives the meat a spoiled taste."

At the end of a regular workday, River would skin the animals and stretch them on the appropriate-sized stretcher boards. Then the hide was placed over the stretcher with the skin-side exposed to the warm air near the wood-burning stove for 12 to 18 hours.

At dawn, the skin was turned, putting the fur on the outside, with the dry skin against the board. This was called "turning the hide," and was done with two purposes in mind. One, so it would slide easily off the board and not stick, and two, so the fur buyer could examine and grade the fur's quality and luster.

There was a distinct odor in the cabins because of the skins. But the odor was worth it, because the furs brought in the money that allowed him to continue living in the Bush. Each fur brought different prices, depending on the size of the pelt, market conditions, quality of fur, time of year caught, and care and preparation given the finished pelt. Dark marten pelts brought the highest price. Only Kuskokwim marten brought a higher price than Talkeetna marten.

A fox was particularly valuable because the fur could bring as much as 80 dollars. It had been pretty discouraging when an animal got away, because that meant the loss of a great deal of money. Sixty dollars had gone a long way toward buying supplies for the winter.

It had been a tremendous amount of hard work, but living in Alaska was hard, by any stretch of the imagination. It wasn't as if he could walk across the street to a Wal-Mart and pick up ready-made traps or the bait for the traps, he further explained to Sharon.

"I never thought about that. So you had to make your own bait, too?"

"Right. Catch and prepare it."

River had often used spruce hen wings as attractors. They not only emitted a savory smell to the marten but also served as a great visual attractor. Spruce hens are mostly found in or near spruce trees, and there are usually 10 to 20 in a flock. He learned by trial and error that if he shot the one on the top branch first, that bird would fall into the others and they would all fly away. So he shot the one on the bottom branch first, and the rest would remain motionless, because staying still was their natural tendency to avoid being spotted. Starting at the bottom, it had been easy to move up the tree, picking them off one at a time.

He said, "I would cut the breast out for food and then prepare the rest of the bird for bait. I placed the discarded scraps in a tightly sealed bag over the stove for about a week, making sure the temperature stayed a consistent 140 degrees."

River paused, waiting for Sharon to question his ability to keep the temperature at a steady level, and was not disappointed because Sharon immediately asked, "How did you maintain that temperature?"

He laughed, and said, "I was just kidding about the temperature part. Wanted to see if you were paying attention."

Sharon punched him in the arm again and said, "I'm going to stop believing everything you say, if you aren't careful."

"But you are so fun to tease," he said and gave her a quick kiss.

He explained that he took the bag outside, where the temperature often ranged from 20 to 40 below, and left it. The remains of the spruce hens froze solid. When he needed bait, he would cut off the plastic bag, place the frozen chunk on a stump and use an axe to chop it into two-inch cubes. Marten and other furbearers could smell the thawing, rotten spruce hens from up to a mile away. With any luck they would be lured into his traps.

Sharon could not comprehend why anyone would risk life and limb while working themselves to the bone if they didn't have to.

"Why did you do all that?"

"Because I needed the bait for my traps," River simply answered.

"No, not that. The whole thing. Why did you live out there and risk your life? I could understand if you were living in the 1800s or early 1900s, when people didn't have a choice. You chose to shun modern conveniences that were available to you 30 years ago. You didn't have to live like that. What made you do it?"

"I did it because of something my mother taught me. I could be anything I wanted, if I was willing to work hard for it."

"Mother Shirley is a very wise woman," Sharon agreed. "She must be very proud of you, because you have really put her words of advice into practice."

"I hope so. Thanks to her, I had the fortitude to put in the time and effort, plus I really liked the lifestyle, not because I just wanted to make a living. I had to live somewhere, and I really wanted my life to make a difference.

"And I did it because of the attitude of indifference people seemed to have when I returned from India. I found people were nonchalant and disinterested, even oblivious to what was going on in the rest of the world. I was thoroughly disillusioned by that.

"There is always passion found in survival, and subsistence living draws people closer to nature and one another. Yes, it is dangerous, because a lot of the people in the 70s were like Elvis Presley's song, *Caught in a Trap*; a life built on wants and materialism and not needs. It just wasn't fulfilling to me."

"I understand that part, but how did you find the courage to do it?"

"It is more about desire than courage. It was a way to escape the type of life I wasn't attracted to. I wanted a simpler life."

"What you did out there and how you lived doesn't seem simple to me. It seems extremely complicated and difficult."

"Then consider this: I had the need to be free and independent; to not have to rely on others, like the telephone and electricity companies, grocery stores and car dealerships. It seemed everyone was busy trying to make a profit off everyone else. I just wanted to live."

"I can understand that," Sharon recalled, drifting into thought.

She recalled staring at death in the eyes of that demon bear, and how nothing mattered to her but living and being able to see her family again.

"So, these skills that you learned while walking the traplines along the Susitna River taught you that?" Sharon asked.

"Yep. It also taught me how to approach the Lower 48 business world. You see, farming experiences taught me how to cope with life in the wilderness. Living in the wilderness trained me to be a skilled riverboater. Every day was another hard lesson, but eventually the difficult lessons connected me to a rhythm with life."

"And you think that all that learning contributed to your current business success?"

"I do, and I keep coming back to those basics. Being successful in trapping is all about learning the mindset of the animal. We've already talked a lot about this in our marketing brainstorming, but to reiterate—animals, like people, will take the path of least resistance and what is relevant to how they live. Marten live in trees and beavers live in the water. Learn their habits, feeding patterns, and what makes them tick. The acquired knowledge and skills will eventually carry over into whatever industry you work, even riverboat services."

"So, that's how you approached the travel industry business, isn't it? It paid off on the river, the same way it paid off on the traplines of the wilderness."

River nodded yes, obviously pleased that she understood.

"I can see how you were thinking. You asked yourself, what were the habits of the people who traveled to Alaska? You learned their habits and later used it to market your products."

"That's right," River replied. "You can have the best product, but if you don't market it well, you will fail. What are the lifestyles of the people you are trying to attract? Look at television advertising. Would you try to attract hunters and fishermen during a children's program? The people who want to come to Alaska, what are they watching? Even if it costs more money, you will get more return on your investment if you advertise during the news, weather, sports, or financial channels."

River continued thinking along these lines and rationalized that some men would find a way to cope with anything, and the smart ones would build upon what they learned. This knowledge had worked on the farm in New York, and in the impoverished fields of India. It paid off in the freezing temperatures of the wilderness, and now in the competitive business world of a changing Alaska.

He squeezed Sharon's hand and said, "It paid off in trapping a wife, too." They both laughed.

He added, "And it will work in trapping The Big One," he said in a somber, almost inaudible tone.

Sharon wondered, was it mostly luck or skill he needed? Destiny had been good to him, perhaps because he had been willing to pay the price for his dreams, often at the risk of his own life. Was fate on his side this time? Only time would tell, but for now, the train was pulling into Talkeetna, and it was time to disembark. Mike should be waiting for them at the station, since they had called him from the trail.

"So, what are you going to do now?" Sharon asked. "Your frontier is disappearing."

"There's always a frontier. I think I'd make a good space explorer."

"Living on the moon, now, huh? You should have discussed this with me before the wedding."

They laughed, and River pointed out that priorities had definitely changed. "Now, I'm fighting over cell phone bills. I sometimes think life was easier in the wilderness."

Suddenly, seeing a familiar face, he said, "There's Mike. You are saved from hearing more stories." They both laughed and waved at Mike.

"Hey you two," said Mike. "Did the boat break down? Why are you on the train?"

"No, the boat is fine. We just had a little adventure."

Sharon's eyes showed an expression of disbelief. "Little adventure? We were almost killed by two bears and one of them was The Big One."

## Chapter Twelve
# Who's Hunting Whom?

Several people nearby were startled when they heard The Big One mentioned. They stopped and anxiously looked at Sharon, wanting to hear more.

River noticed the fearful looks and said loudly to Mike and Sharon, "True, we did see a couple of bears, but they were too small to be The Big One."

Sharon quickly realized what was going on. River didn't want to panic anyone, and poor Mike was checking out their faces, trying to decide whether or not this was some kind of a joke.

After getting out of earshot, River apologized to Sharon, who said, "I forgive you. When I saw the looks on the faces of the people around us, I figured out what was going on."

"She's right, though," River confided to Mike. "It was The Big One. We were up at my old cabin, and Sharon was inside, when a huge grizzly was suddenly in the doorway, about to have her for dinner. We thought it was The Big One. I was behind, in my old workshop, and couldn't get a killing shot."

Mike was staring at them in amazement, still not sure whether or not they were teasing him. Logically thinking, he realized that for River to leave a boat unattended, something terrible had to have happened.

River continued. "I was trying to reposition for a killing shot when another grizzly came charging out of the woods and went straight for the bear in the doorway. The two bears locked into a ferocious fight, and tumbled down the ridge. We decided it was time to get out of Dodge and took the old trail to Peter's cabin in the opposite direction from the fighting bears."

Sharon shivered all over again thinking about the encounter, and added, "We were backtracking to the boat when the train came by, so we called you and hopped on."

Mike whistled and shook his head in disbelief. "Something has got to be done soon. That sounds too close for comfort. First, though, why don't we take one of the boats and recover the one you left."

"Yeah, that would be great."

"You're not going without me," Sharon piped in. She knew River had something up his sleeve to ditch her, and go track those bears.

"Sharon," River tried to softly reason with her, "I'm not going to go after the bears tonight, but in case they do show up, I don't want you there. Do you want to face him again?"

"No," Sharon admitted. "But can you honestly promise me that you aren't going after him? Besides, it's getting late, and we're supposed to meet Don in a couple of hours."

"Israel and I can go get the boat," Mike offered.

"Why can't I ride with you and stay on Mike's boat?" Sharon asked. "We should be back in plenty of time to meet Don, if you are being honest with me."

"What am I going to do with her, Mike?" River sighed while shaking his head. He squeezed Sharon's hand and, looking at her, tried to send a mental message that if anything happened to her, well, he didn't even want to consider it.

"Think you already did it," Mike replied, answering River's question. "You married her."

They all laughed, and Sharon said, "I'll take that as a yes."

So in just a few minutes, Mike, River and a victorious Sharon were in the boat, heading back to where they had left the other boat. They were deep in thought and grateful that the loud roar of the engine blocked out the possibility of meaningless but polite conversation.

Mike was thinking about the possibility of running into The Big One when they arrived at the boat. He was still having a difficult time believing this dangerous encounter and was glad no one got hurt.

River was strategizing how to go after The Big One without Sharon finding out.

Sharon was wondering, *What am I doing, going back out there where Big Bear and Demon are waiting? I'm not Annie Oakley.*

Eventually, they reached the place where River and Sharon had tied up the boat. Mike stayed offshore with Sharon, while they all scanned the area for bear sign.

From their location on the river, they were close enough to see that the boat appeared safe. River picked up his binoculars and glassed the area.

Once River was sure everything was safe, he jumped ashore, untied the boat and took off downriver with Mike and Sharon close behind. All were relieved to have no further encounters with bears, but River did not tell them that he had found huge bear prints inside the boat.

Sharon wondered when River would go after The Big One. Time

was running out. Hibernation was imminent. Bears would be disappearing soon, and then return in the spring. She knew River was right. He had to do something, but why did it have to be him? Couldn't someone else handle this situation?

At least tomorrow they would be on the river all day, doing the new Devils Canyon Tour for the travel agents who could send a substantial amount of business to Mahay's Riverboat Service next summer.

"I sure hope Big Bear doesn't show up tomorrow," she said out loud, and Mike laughed because it was the first time he had heard her reference to The Big One.

"Yeah, me too," Mike agreed. "We certainly don't need to see him tomorrow. You two were fortunate. You know that, don't you?"

"I do, but I don't think River does. He just saw it as another day in the life of Daniel Boone."

Mike laughed. "But he's right, Sharon. You've got to see that."

"I do, Mike. What I don't see why he has to take care of this? And if you say because it's *The Mahay Way,* I'll scream."

"Okay, I won't say it … but you know it's true. Were you thinking of some other reason?"

"Kind of … but it seems very strange and I'm almost afraid to say it out loud."

"What is it?" Mike pressed.

"It's that bear, Mike. It's like he's been following us and tracking us, much like River used to trap animals. The Big One saved my life out there today, and I don't think he's stalking River. It's that other bear, the one I call Demon. I was never so scared in my entire life, nor have I ever seen such eyes of hatred. He looked at me as if he totally despised me, like it was a personal vendetta, or something."

"It is. You're part of his food chain," Mike suggested.

"I know, but it just seems more than that. I can't logically explain it, because it makes no sense. But having looked into his eyes, I'm more afraid for River. Who is hunting whom here? I know he could handle one bear but there are two of them now, and although they seem to dislike one another, I feel as if they are also aware that time is running out. And I don't know anything about trapping animals, but I've seen what men will do when they are backed into a corner."

"You have a point there," Mike agreed. "No one likes being backed into a corner, and I imagine not even bears."

"I'm thinking especially bears," Sharon sighed, and they both settled back to complete the short river ride back to the dock.

River was thinking along the same lines as he led the way in his boat. His many years of living off the land gave him the opportunity to understand what it feels like to be hunted.

# Chapter Thirteen
# The Fairview Inn

River and Sharon hurried home to change clothes. They had less than an hour before meeting Don. River stood in the shower with the warm water massaging the strong muscles in his back.

*This sure would have felt good after some of those hikes around Clear Creek,* he thought. *Especially after that time I was lost.* He hadn't thought about those experiences for many years and telling Sharon about them had released a flood of memories.

Seeing the cabins, riding the train, remembering stories, and now about to meet Don was like stepping back in time. He remembered one particular time when he traveled to the inn, many years back. He'd been definitely in need of some human companionship, conversation, and a beer.

He recalled the lonely feeling while traveling swiftly across the snow toward town. The world looked much larger when covered with deep white snow and he was a lone figure in the dark. He could even still imagine the crisp sound of the runners on the hard-packed snow. It was the only sound that could be heard.

The dogsled was made up of five well-trained dogs excited to be running again. As a musher, River knew to intently watch the movements and behaviors of the dogs for signs of nearby wolves or moose. Just crossing a trail where one of these animals had crossed would cause the dogs to become jittery and nervous. A smart musher could know in advance if he was about to run into trouble.

It was 40 below in the dead of winter, so there were only a few hours of daylight. Suddenly, River saw something in the sky he had never seen before and the memory of it still gave him the shivers. There was a point of green light, like a star, but brighter. He watched it grow larger and larger, forming a perfect, giant-green smoke ring, and then it dispersed. It was as if something unbelievable had come into the atmosphere, letting him know how small and insignificant he was.

*I need to remember to tell Sharon about that some time.* Then he turned off the water and quickly dried off. She was applying the finishing touches to her makeup and he quietly watched, amazed at her beauty.

"You can't improve on perfection," he said.

"Why, thank you. I want to look my best since I'm excited to be going out with two handsome guys."

"And I'm excited to be with you, anywhere."

"Wow. You are certainly charming tonight."

"I'm still remembering that kiss on the train today."

"Well, there might be more where that came from," she said.

"I'm counting on it." He took her in his arms.

"Hate to change the subject," Sharon whispered through a contented smile, "but we are going to be late."

"I don't care."

But they separated and both rushed to finish getting ready, and then hurried to the car to drive the short distance to town. After the danger of what had happened at the cabin, it was amazing that they were both in such high spirits and full of revitalized energy at the thought of going out.

River again remembered the story of the green lights in the sky and described the experience to Sharon, who was fascinated.

"I felt really spooked, and ran the dogs harder to get into town faster. I had seen it once before, but couldn't share it with anyone, because it was just too weird and they would start to wonder about me."

"You mean, they didn't wonder about you before?" Sharon asked.

"Well, they probably did, but I didn't want to make it worse."

"Good point, but, seriously, wasn't it just the northern lights?"

"No. I had seen them hundreds of times, but this was very different."

"Did you ever find out what it was?"

"No, I never did. I was so spooked, I didn't even care if I had dinner with the infamous grouch."

"Now I know you're pulling my leg."

"No I'm not. It's all true."

"There really was a grouch?"

"I'm sure there was more than one, but only one in particular claimed the title."

"No way," Sharon said. "Who was it?"

"It was the postmaster, Major Kirkman. He was drunk most of the time, and hated hippies. Mike had long hair back then, and when he went to pick up his mail, knowing he had some, the Major insisted he didn't have any. He was really grumpy. Everyone in town used him as a grouch-measuring stick. You knew you had been alone in the Bush too long, or the darkness was getting to you, if you were beginning to act like him. It was his only claim to fame."

"You're making this up," Sharon said.

"Ask Mike."

"I'm going to," Sharon promised.

People went to the Fairview Inn for warmth and friendship, to overcome cabin fever, to hear all the new stories of legends and lore, or to entertain one another with accounts of death-defying animal attacks, engine failures, locations of cabins, trails, resources for river travel, the location of a mean, wounded grizzly, and other necessary survival wisdom. It was smart to go there and listen.

Others went to tell their near-death experiences, or to report who died or had a baby, who left whom, how duct tape was used to temporarily close up wounds from a recent bear mauling, how a pair of Carhartt pants saved a life, the latest weather predictions, and maybe even where The Big One was last sighted.

Sharon said, "Maybe we should have gone to the inn before visiting your cabin today. We might have learned in advance that The Big One and Demon Eyes were hanging out there. Are we going to share our recent sighting?"

"I don't think so," River answered.

"Why not?" Sharon asked.

"I don't think it would help the situation. It would probably just perpetuate the panic."

Sharon agreed he was right. Remembering the stories he had told her on the train, she asked, "Did you share your cable and prospector's cabin discoveries?"

"Absolutely. I told the townsfolk in case someone else needed to use them. Knowing these things could mean the difference between life and death for someone. That's just the way it's done here."

"At the time, it seems the Fairview Inn was undoubtedly one of the most important stops in town," Sharon said.

"It really was. Plus, it was important to stop there before picking up any supplies, because you could find out the going prices, which was a good thing to know before any bartering began. All in all, it was just a great way to measure the community temperature while becoming acclimated into redeveloping some lost social manners and graces."

"Which were probably deeply in need."

"Deeply."

The Fairview Inn was built by Ben Nauman around 1921. Many different people owned the inn over the years, but the townsfolk would never stop thinking of the inn as belonging only to Talkeetna.

It had been the gathering place for locals as well as visitors, and had the honor of having the first bathtub in the area. This created tremendous feelings of respect from the residents, and humor in those passing through from the Lower 48.

A ruling was passed that no other building on the two-block-long Main Street could be built taller than the 28.5-foot-tall Fairview Inn. The inn was the nerve center of the village, and it behooved an individual to spend some time there before heading out into the Bush.

There were only six rooms available to rent, and one of them, the Green Room, is said to be haunted by President Warren G. Harding. He spent the night there in 1923 on his way to San Francisco, after visiting Alaska to drive the Golden Spike for the Alaska Railroad. Local myths say it was food poisoning, while others say someone intentionally poisoned him because he was an unpopular president. (He actually suffered a heart attack outside Alaska.) Apparently, the inn enjoyed the notoriety and wanted to take a little of the credit.

"Some residents and guests claim that they have seen his ghost in the Green Room, and books have even been written about it," River said.

"You don't strike me as the sort of person who believes in ghosts," Sharon pointed out.

"Fact is stranger than fiction," River raised his eyebrows and smiled, making a deep, evil-sounding laugh.

Sharon laughed at the face he was making, and said, "I'm beginning to question the veracity of your stories."

"Madame Mahay, I seldom pull your leg, unless I'm serious."

"That's the problem. I can't tell when you're serious. Besides, I've never heard of anyone wanting to take credit for poisoning someone, or wanting to have the title of a grouch."

"But this is Alaska, my dear."

They had a good laugh thinking about poor old President Harding and mean old Major Kirkman, as they pulled into the parking space on the side of the inn.

"I'm in serious need of another kiss from my wife," River said, before getting out of the car. Sharon seriously complied. They eventually walked into the Fairview Inn where they were shown to a table for three and waited for Don to arrive.

(above) Large sign at a park entrance in Alaska, reminding visitors that "A Fed Bear is a Dead Bear."

(left) City sign at the entrance of the village of Talkeetna, Alaska.

(below) Baby moose seen off the back porch of the Mahay's current home.

*(right) Director of Adventure Tours, Mahay's Riverboat Services: Sandi Mischenko.*

*(above) A jetboat snagged in a logjam on the Talkeetna River. River rescued the survivors.*

*(right) Nagley's Store, downtown Talkeetna.*

*The famous Fairview Inn, in downtown Talkeetna.*

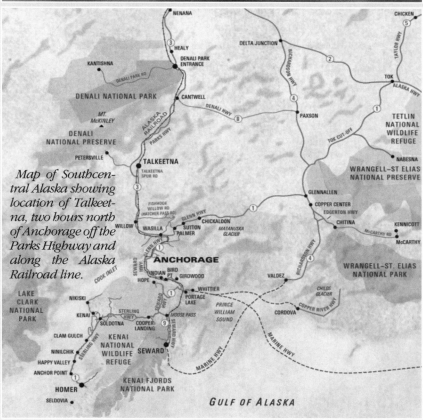

*Map of Southcentral Alaska showing location of Talkeetna, two hours north of Anchorage off the Parks Highway and along the Alaska Railroad line.*

*(right) Preacher River Mahay performing the wedding ceremony of Lisa and Jacque in Talkeetna, September, 2006.*

*(below) Mike and Mary Stewart. Mike is the Director of Operations at Mahay's Riverboat Service.*

*(below) The modern, current home of Steve and Sharon Mahay, not built by Steve, but still 10 miles outside of Talkeetna, off a main road, not a bear path.*

(top) Original Mahay farm in Saratoga Lake, north of Albany, New York.

(above) Steve Mahay at 11 years old in his fifth-grade school picture.

(above right) Always happy 18-month-old Steve Mahay, in Saratoga Springs, New York.

(right) Steve Mahay (right) presenting arms and demonstrating the proper handling and cleaning techniques for 4-H Club in 1962.

*(above) Four-year-old Israel Mahay painted to look like a river pirate.*

*(right) Newspaper article about 19-year-old Stephen Mahay who was accepted as a volunteer to Peace Corp India Project # 34.*

*(middle) Steve Mahay (second from the left) in India teaching the locals to develop irrigation systems and how to properly fertilize their farmlands.*

## Named Volunteer For Peace Corps

STEPHEN MAHAY

SCHUYLERVILLE — St Mahay has been named a Corps volunteer after con ing eight weeks of trainii State University of New at Albany and five weeks country training in India.

Mr. Mahay is one of than 500 volunteers trained summer and fall to aid in I food production and nut program. Mr. Mahay's gro 80 left for India Oct. 21 have now been assigned t lages in the northern stat Uttar Pradesh, Punjab an jasthan. The volunteers work in general agricultur tension, food production community leadership de ment work.

During their training a bany, the volunteers studie Hindi language, Indian h and culture, U.S. history world affairs. Technical ing included practical wo agricultural extension me poultry production and co tive management.

With this group's arrival 1,050 volunteers will be at in India. Besides agricu Peace Corps projects the clude education, rural

*(below) Steve Mahay and his three sons Israel, Noah and Judah in their log cabin in the village of Talkeetna, in 1982.*

*(left) Steve Mahay with Judah, Noah and Israel at Hatcher Pass in the Talkeetna Mountain Range, in 1983.*

*(middle) Steve Mahay, mother Shirley Mahay VanArnum and stepdad, Vern.*

*(lower left) The wedding day of Sharon and Steve Mahay in New York on April 9, 2005.*

*(lower right) Sharon Heim Mahay and her mother, Darleen Heim.*

115

(right) Israel, Judah and Noah at the wedding of Sharon and Steve Mahay.

(left) A proud dad: Captain Steve Mahay, relaxing with Israel and Judah Mahay at Judah's wedding in 2006.

(below) Darleen Heim and Sharon's brother, Paul Heim.

(left) Israel Mahay (oldest of three sons) with fiancée Kelly.

(below) A very happy Steve and Sharon Mahay at the wedding of son Judah and Lorien Mahay.

*Judah Mahay (middle son) with his new bride, Lorien.*

*Steve and Sharon Mahay traveling in the Lower 48.*

*Kris Mahay peeling logs for the first wilderness cabin 10 miles up the Susitna River.*

*Kris Mahay working on the cabin. The cache in the background was always built first to protect food and other valuables from bears.*

*Steve Mahay, who never used a chain saw while building the Susitna River cabin, is shown using his axe to notch a log for placement.*

Making progress, working to beat the winter and have a warm, safe place to live.

The pup tent was home while building the Susitna River cabin.

More progress now showing the cooking stove that was packed up on Steve's back.

*The cabin-building process was slow and tedious using only an axe. This photo shows Mahay's dog, Brute, keeping guard, and clothes drying on a line behind the cabin.*

*The Susitna River cabin is finished. Here is the back view showing the installed glass windows.*

*The split-log front door is finally completed, keeping out the weather and animals. It took two full days to make.*

*The finished Susitna River cabin in October, 1975, with its sod roof and dirt floor. This was the Mahay home for five years.*

*The proud Mahay couple standing in the doorway of their warm, comfortable home during the first winter out in the wilderness.*

*A new snowfall brings a visit from the Stanleys' dog.*

*A much later visit in 1985 to the Susitna River cabin by Steve, Kris and Israel Mahay.*

*Another visitor in 1985: Christopher Stanley, son of Peter and Ginny Stanley.*

*Twenty years later, the Susitna River cabin still stands. Bears have broken in and trashed it, while native plants have almost overtaken it.*

Peter Stanley (left) and Steve Mahay (right) pulling a felled log for Peter's cabin, 1972.

Peter and Ginny Stanley's completed cabin, just over the hill from the Mahay's cabin.

Peter and Ginny Stanley standing in the doorway of their cabin, 1974, and then 30 years later, 2004.

*(above) The Cat-train seismic crew (north of the Brooks Range) preparing to relocate.*

*(middle) Seismic Cat-train on the move, north of the Brooks Range and south of the Arctic Ocean.*

*(inset) Nodwell drill operated by Steve Mahay in the early days of working on the North Slope.*

*(bottom) Cat-train in the Brooks Range, carrying the seismic crew on the North Slope, including Steve Mahay.*

*Steve Mahay skinning a bear, while Brute keeps an eye out for intruders.*

*Bears provided excellent fresh meat for sustenance. This is a large black bear hide stretched on the right side of the front of the Susitna River cabin.*

*(above) Author Deborah Cox Wood with Steve Mahay at the Susitna River cabin. (inset) Chris Batin and author Deborah Cox Wood taking a break from working on* The Legend of River Mahay. *(bottom) Judah Mahay and other hunters at another line cabin used for trapping on the Talkeetna River, in 1997.*

# Chapter Fourteen
# Planes and Boats

Don Lee was a local pilot for Talkeetna Aero Services. River had met him around 1974. He had also been a hunting and fishing guide, so an instant friendship had formed. Later Don started a charter floatplane business and had worked as a commercial pilot in Talkeetna for over 28 years. Thinking about Don stirred up memories for River regarding their many near-death experiences when flying. They were fortunate to still be alive. It was hard to think of flying without thinking of Don.

It was unusual to have a crisis involving a plane without Don being in the picture, but this was one of those times. River had witnessed a serious plane crash out in the middle of nowhere.

A Super Cub pilot, Dennis Brown, flew River and his two hunting companions, Dennis and Walter, one at a time to a remote gravel bar on the Yentna River. They hiked quite a distance over difficult and rough terrain where they shot two beautiful bull moose.

Packing out more than 1,000 pounds of meat would have been a tremendous amount of hard work. Dennis decided to hike back and fly the Cub to an open area near them to pick up the downed moose.

Much to the hunters' horror, they watched the plane touch down and immediately flip over. Dennis was hanging upside down in the cockpit, alive, but with aviation fuel leaking everywhere. He was obviously shook up, but not seriously hurt, and was able to extricate himself from the wreckage. Now they were faced with a greater dilemma: They needed to be rescued.

Soon, a small plane appeared overhead. The hunters decided to lie flat on their backs, with arms and legs outstretched, which had been recommended on the back of their hunting licenses as a signal to use if in distress. River said to his companions while lying on the terrain, "Let's hope the pilot reads the back of his license and figures out why we're doing this."

The plane left the area and about two hours later a helicopter from Elmendorf Air Force Base picked them up and flew back to Talk-eetna. Because firearms were not allowed on board the helicopter, the group had to leave all their gear, then find a way to get back to the site. A Super Cub was the only type of plane that could land on that particular gravel bar, so they contacted two local Cub pilots.

The pilots dropped them off at the original landing spot, along with necessary supplies to repair the plane and start packing out the moose. At the crash site they decided to flip over the plane and see if the engine would run.

In order to turn the plane over, the logical thing to do was dig a hole underneath the plane, at least six feet deep and long enough to pivot the plane on the wing's axis. Hopefully, this would allow it to completely turn over, and bring it back to the upright position.

Amazingly, the plan worked with no further damage to the plane. This had not been an easy thing to do, because although the tundra was not frozen, it was hard and rocky. Unfortunately, after they flipped it over, they discovered a severe bend in the last 10 inches of propeller. The prop might still be stable enough to rotate and fly the plane if they could cut off the damaged 10 inches with a hacksaw.

They cut it off and hoped for the best. Dennis checked the fuel level and there was enough to fly. The moment of truth came when the engine sputtered several times, kicked in, and ran smoothly.

They pushed the plane back into the brush as far as it would go, which helped create a longer runway. Fortunately, there was a slight downhill slope. The makeshift runway was 50 yards of open field with tall grass, followed by 10 yards of four-foot-high willow brush and finally a cliff.

Dennis revved up the engine while standing on the brakes, so the plane wouldn't move forward until the right moment. He gave the hand signal to get ready, then released the brake. All three hunters began running down the grassy field, pushing on the wings and tail as hard as they could. Soon the plane was traveling faster than they could run. By the time Dennis reached the cliff, the plane was supposed to have picked up enough ground speed to become airborne, and they were happy as it continued to pick up speed as it reached the willows.

Their joy was short lived when the prop cut up the thick willow brush and sent it sailing over the fuselage, keeping the plane from reaching the necessary airspeed. The plane nosedived off the cliff, and seconds later, instead of seeing the plane become airborne, they heard a crash.

River, Dennis and Walter half-ran, half-stumbled to the cliff's edge.

Peering over, they saw a deep ravine with huge boulders at the bottom, and a busted-up plane among them. No one figured Dennis could be alive, but after climbing down, they found that he had miraculously survived without serious injury.

The four of them hiked to the prearranged pickup place designated earlier by the two pilots who had dropped them off. The pilots showed up on time and flew them back to Talkeetna. Later, Dennis contracted a helicopter to airlift his crashed plane back to town, and eventually he rebuilt the airplane in his garage.

The sad part of the story was that their two moose had rotted, and they lost all the meat. This was not what River would call a good hunt.

"Sharon," River said, bringing his thoughts back to the present, "did you know Don Lee was part of the aerial support during the filming of the Devils Canyon run? He followed overhead while giving a narrative on how I was progressing. He was my eyes-in-the-sky."

"Really? I didn't know that was Don's voice," Sharon said.

River was grateful to be able to relax. In the past, he had dealt with near-death experiences almost daily, his own as well as those of others, but today's bear confrontation had left him exhausted. Perhaps it was because he was older, but immediately discounted that argument. *It had to be over my concern for Sharon.* They had been fortunate. *What was going on with those bears?* He had never seen or heard of anything like this before.

Sharon was also thinking about how good it felt to relax at the inn and she made a mental note to listen carefully. People around her might provide important information that she might use or need in the future. She didn't think a cable crossing or cabin location, however, would be pertinent to her existence. *More like, where are the good sales?*

"I wonder where Don is?" she asked. "Do you think he forgot?"

"I don't think so. We are actually a little early."

Suddenly Don walked in, spotted them and quickly moved to their table.

"Hey, River and Sharon." Don shook hands with River and hugged Sharon. He pulled up a chair and ordered a drink.

"Really good to see you two. We haven't done this in a long time. Too long. Seems like we had more time to hang out with people we cared about when we were poor."

"Or we made the time," River said. "I never thought of us as being poor."

"Well I guess we weren't really," Don agreed. "It didn't take much to live on back then and we had all the moose and salmon we could eat. In reality, there was an abundance of everything we needed."

"There was," River said. They sat quietly for a moment, contemplating this irony of life.

Sharon said, "Don, what have you been up to, lately."

"Not much. Getting old and working. What's new with you two?"

"About the same. I took Sharon to see the old cabin today."

"Yes he did. And he told me that it was just a short hike along a well-marked trail. The short hike turned out to be several miles, uphill, and the well-marked trail was a bear path."

They knew she was not exaggerating, and River winked at Sharon, thinking about their experience at the cabin.

"Speaking of bears, Sharon, did you know that if you and a friend come upon a bear, you don't have to be able to run fast, just faster than your friend?"

Don had no idea how much his statement impacted Sharon, especially after the bear encounters that had taken place earlier that day. What he said was also having a healing effect on them. Don was good medicine and continued to entertain with his bear anecdotes.

"If you have a small gun, you just shoot the other person in the foot, and they scream like a 12-year-old girl, which attracts the bear. Then you quickly remove yourself from the area."

They hooted with laughter.

"Speaking of bears," River said, "did you hear that several of them went through town and hit all the trash cans?"

"I did hear that." Then he turned and explained to Sharon. "You can easily tell the difference between a dog or a bear hitting a trash can. A dog will pull out a few things he wants to eat, but a bear will knock over a trash can and spread the contents all over, because they are very curious. They will also bite into everything."

Sharon thought of the trashed cabin, and had to agree. Everything had been chewed on and scattered. It reminded her of a game her older brother, Paul, had suckered her into as a kid. It was called 52-Card Pickup. He threw the cards all over the room and she had to pick them up.

"They even bite airplanes," Don continued. "Three black bear cubs were recently on the wings of one of my planes, with sharp claws that tore them to shreds. Bears are creatures of habit and my plane was parked on their trail. They walked to and over it, refusing to go around. If there is salmon in the plane or float compartment, they bite through the metal. The teenage bears are the worst and won't stop for anything. I've seen them go right through the side of a plane. But, did you know there is a bear coalition now in town?"

"We heard that," answered Sharon.

"They call themselves the *Bear Necessities*. They are trying to educate people to live in harmony with the bears, because a bear that gets too close is a dead one. Now I'm a pacifist and help relocate the animals. I've really become soft in my old age. I won't fly out people from the Lower 48 anymore who just want to kill something."

"So, are you a vegetarian?" Sharon asked.

"No. I still like to eat moose meat, but it's a lot of work to track, shoot and clean them."

River said, "Yeah, it's easy to pull the trigger, but the real work begins after that. It's gruesome, messy and time-consuming. I am cleaning one right now in the garage. I put the head outside and a bear got it."

"Must have been a big bear," Don said.

Sharon looked up to hear River's answer. "Around 400 pounds."

"Man, just a puppy. We've seen a lot of bears over the years, haven't we?" Don reminisced. "We came out here during a pioneering time. It was all Bush planes then, and jetboats weren't around yet. I found a niche with planes and you, obviously, found a niche with boats. Have you shown Sharon your first flatboat?"

"Yes, he did," Sharon said. "It's in the boat burial ground."

"You still thinking of resurrecting it?" Don teased.

"Of course. I'm thinking about planting flowers in it and placing it on the roof of the front office." Nothing was ever wasted in Alaska.

"I heard you had some plane trouble recently," River said.

"I did. My plane went into aerodynamic flutter, and started to fall apart at 11,000 feet. The only thing I could do at that point was slow down and hope for the best, knowing that if you go down in some areas of Alaska, you're dead. Pretty simple. Fortunately, I slowed down and was able to land safely. Nothing's changed about living in the Bush: Lots of boredom, interrupted by moments of sheer terror."

"Sharon, did River tell you any stories about when he did a little prospecting, always secretly trying to find the mother lode?"

"I heard he had done some prospecting, but he assures me that he doesn't have any gold hidden away."

"I believe that, but as I recall, he had staked out some claims once up in the Talkeetna Mountains. I flew him and another guy and their shovels to an old expired gold claim filed by some guy named Capps, who had been a government surveyor. I dropped them off 80 miles from the nearest road, where no one ever goes. I tried to land on a gravel bar, but discovered it wasn't a good idea because the brush grabbed my landing gear and took us down. Caused some damage, but no one got hurt. Did you find any gold?"

"What do you think?" River asked. "I'll bet you would have remembered if I did. Capp's site was right in the middle of a bunch of alders, but since there was no water, we couldn't pan to find out if there was any gold. We gave up and never went back."

"Figures," said Don. "Guess nothing terribly exciting happened except for our bad landing."

"I've always heard that any landing you can walk away from is a good landing," Sharon said.

"Well, then most of mine have been good," Don said.

There was one where he didn't walk away. Don had been seriously injured after he pancaked a plane in the exact same place another plane had just crashed.

When the rescue helicopter arrived, with River as the EMT, they were shocked to find two planes instead of one. They came to his plane with a body bag and found Don and his co-pilot alive. The two in the other plane, however, had perished. It had taken Don years to recover from the accident because his back was broken with multiple compression fractures. Indeed, an injury such as this took a long time to heal.

"I found River a couple of times, stranded out there on the river. And once with eight senior Holland America people on board."

"That's right," River said. "I forgot you were the one who found us. You tipped a wing, and went for help."

"Yep. I saw you down there walking around on a gravel bar, and asked myself why you had parked there. You knew better than that. We only had citizen band radios back then, and no cell phones. Of course, River didn't have one. So I called back to town to tell them he was okay, but stuck on a gravel bar. They soon sent another boat after him."

Sharon had not heard this story before and asked, "What happened?"

"We were going downstream in the Talkeetna Canyon, headed for the canyon wall with Class-IV whitewater, when the steering controls locked up and I truly thought we were going to die. There was nothing that could be done to prevent from crashing into the 200-foot-high rock wall.

"It was ironic that they were laughing, drinking hot chocolate and coffee, totally unaware we were about to die. I shouted, 'Brace yourselves, we're going to crash!' They were smart and listened."

River remembered how he had placed his feet on the control panel, something boaters would normally never do. It was imperative to always protect the instruments, but knowing there wasn't any hope, he didn't want to die by flying through the windshield.

Seconds later, the boat slammed into the rock wall, the metal hull crunching like a soda can under foot. He wondered why the river that had sustained him for so long was now trying to claim his life.

"So what happened?" Sharon asked. "And don't tell me you died." Everyone was aware of the Mahay sense of humor.

"No, I didn't die, nor was I even afraid to meet my Maker. But the boat was sinking, and I wasn't prepared to go that way."

River turned off the engine, opened the cowling and checked for damage. What he saw wasn't pretty. The engine had slammed forward, breaking its mounts and opening the two, three-inch exhaust ports below the water line. The vessel was taking on water and would sink in minutes if he didn't act quickly. He rounded up the passenger's baseball caps and stuffed several into each of the two holes. Everyone was surprised to see that the hats actually stopped the leaks. In checking for injuries, it was amazing that no one was seriously hurt.

River threw out the anchor and everyone put on life jackets. Then they removed the canopy. Overhanging branches, commonly known as sweepers, could snag onto the canopy, flip the boat and sink it. And there were countless sweepers and strainers on the Talkeetna.

The anchor line continued to hold them in a very narrow canyon in the middle of the rapids. After they reached the two-hour-late mark, River knew a rescue boat would soon be looking for them because that had always been the company's emergency plan.

They weren't sinking and felt secure knowing someone would eventually find them. They were comfortable; laughing and joking for about 45 minutes, when disaster struck again. The anchor line broke.

Once again, the boat began to bounce off the canyon walls. River decided to use a technique he teaches to all his captains when a boat loses power in a narrow canyon.

No one liked to do it, because it didn't feel right. He had to get all eight people to stand against the gunnel where the rock wall was going to hit, in order to keep the boat from taking on water.

He explained what to do in a few short words, and they immediately complied. This action—called high siding—actually worked and stopped the upstream side of the vessel from taking on water and sinking them.

River continued to describe the events to Don and Sharon.

"We crashed a couple more times, making it through the canyon before finally drifting safely onto a gravel bar. We secured the boat, thankful to have escaped the canyon rapids."

"So you were saved," said Sharon.

"Well, not really … not yet. Right after that, we heard a plane and saw Don in his Super Cub. I gave him a thumbs-up sign and he radioed base to send another boat."

River had then attempted to prepare everyone for the possibility of having to spend the night out in the cold, open air. They were preparing to build a bonfire when the rescue boat arrived.

They still weren't out of danger because it was essential to have adequate light to safely navigate the 27 miles to the dock. There had never been navigation aids on the Talkeetna River. Safe navigation required the captain to keep the shoreline in sight at all times and identify landmarks, so the captain would always know his position on the river.

River explained, "I felt we had a better-than-fair chance of being able to make it safely back before dark. If there was cloud cover, or any number of reasons, there was a chance they would have to beach the boat on a bar in the remaining light, build a fire in the dark and tough it out until morning. When the choice was put to a vote, it was unanimous to try to go back.

"Forty-five minutes later we successfully docked. We were surprised to see the Holland America tour bus had waited six hours for our return. The driver drove everyone to my home in the village, where hot chili and biscuits were waiting. Then he drove them back to Anchorage."

This event took place in 1982, and River figured he'd never get another client from Holland America. An 80-year-old passenger was the only person who ever mentioned the breakdown to River, saying, "My mother told me I shouldn't go on this trip."

Don said, "You know, I miss those days. Nowadays, there are so many rules that it's amazing anyone can make a living. I think we've lost something that we came out here to find, the freedom to choose how we want to live."

Sharon said, "Don, I heard something you might like. I forgot where, but it went like this: *When a village has no moral principles, laws are ineffective; and when a village has moral principles, laws are not necessary.*"

"I do like that," he replied. "It makes you think about the way the world turns, doesn't it? You know, even though it used to be physically hard to live out here, there were a lot of rewards. Close relationships with people who pulled together to work on projects. Money was definitely a scarce commodity, but we kept gas in the planes and boats, by hook or crook."

River agreed and added, "We worked hard but had a lot of fun over the years. Our original church group created close friendships that have lasted all this time."

Everyone was quiet. Finally, River asked Sharon, "You ready to call it a night?"

"Yes, I've had a great time tonight, but I'm really tired."

"Why don't you walk us to the car, Don."

Once outside, River explained the events of the day. Don lived on a lake near town, and flew his planes all over Alaska. He was always interested in hearing about bear encounters.

Don said, "Thanks for the information. And, by the way, I over-head some guys talking out at the airport today about Chet Bastian. They said he is planning on making a little scene to try and stop your boats from going out on the river anymore."

"Really?" Sharon and River said at the same time. "Like what?"

"Don't know where or when, but he's got some fliers printed up and plans to pass them out to your clients. You know, same old stuff he's been saying."

"If he doesn't back off," Sharon said, "it's going to be him that gets hurt."

River and Don looked at Sharon, dumbfounded.

"What?" she asked.

"Well, well, River. I do believe you have a fighter on your hands," Don said. "Why don't you just let her handle Chet?" They all laughed.

"Thanks for the tip, Don. So far, Bastian has only been making a lot of noise. Guess I better go have a talk with him soon and see if I can straighten this thing out. I do hope, though, for his sake he doesn't pull anything. I'll have to sic Sharon on him."

They all laughed again, said their goodnights and headed home.

# Chapter Fifteen
# The Encampment

The next morning, Sharon and River arrived at the boat dock an hour earlier than the tour group, to make sure nothing was amiss. Don's warning about Chet Bastian did not fall on deaf ears.

"After 31 years, I've seen just about everything that could go wrong, and I don't want anything going wrong today," River said.

Sharon scanned the parking lot and saw nothing out of the ordinary. "It seems all is well," she said. "What can I do to help?"

"Well, we should have plenty of help shortly, but need to wipe the dew off the seats and windows, make sure the P.A. system works, check filters, oil, and sweep the floors."

"Aye, aye, Captain." She saluted and dove into the work at hand.

"Seriously, Sharon. I really appreciate your help on this one. I'm a little nervous about the new tour. Since it's Devils Canyon, well, I just want everyone to love the trip as much as I do."

"They will," Sharon promised, "because of your passion for it. Whatever you do, you are consumed by it, or why do it? Remember?"

"I probably do resemble that remark." They laughed.

Soon several others from the company joined in to help prepare the boat for the day trip. This was to be the first introduction of the new offering, Devils Canyon Tour, and the first time they would be showing a video presentation as part of the tour. It was the Alaska Outdoors September 24, 1985 production of *Devils Canyon: Steve Mahay's Whitewater Challenge*. The 25-minute video had taken second place in a film festival in Nevada. It was Sharon's idea to show it when they stopped to eat lunch at the historic town site of Curry that was adjacent to the Alaska Railroad. They would use a small generator to run the television-video combination. The purpose of showing the video was to build the excitement for their next stop, to experience the inside of Devils Canyon, which was called the Mount Everest of whitewater.

"Here they come," said Sharon when she saw the bus pull into the parking lot. "Everything you love is here today, the tourists, the river, Devils Canyon, and your boat."

"You forgot one thing," River reminded her. "You."

"That goes double for me." She blew him a quick kiss as the first client boarded.

"Welcome aboard," smiled River. "As soon as everyone arrives, we can get started."

Sharon counted heads and indicated that the last person was on board. River turned to the passengers and asked, "How's everyone doing today?"

"Great," they eagerly answered.

"Are you all ready for your Gilligan's Island, three-hour tour?"

Everyone laughed and one man asked, "We are coming back, aren't we?"

"Sure hope so. We'll do our best. Today we have Sharon Mahay, Kelly Marshall, Sandi Mischenko, and myself, River Mahay, to entertain and enlighten you. Did I mention this is my second day on the job?"

The easy laughter was relaxing everyone, including River, and all parties had a feeling this would be a great day. The weather was co-operating. There was a brisk breeze, and the sun was shining, which kept the temperature from falling.

River loved his boats. This one in particular had been specially designed by Darrel Bentz to handle the whitewater of Hell's Canyon on the Snake River. The hull design was perfectly suited for the challenging waters of Devils Canyon. It had three Cummings diesel engines; the jet units were manufactured in Christchurch, New Zealand, and were model 274 Hamilton jets.

The draft of the vessel was approximately 12 inches, with a cruising speed of 35 to 40 mph. Sitting still, it took four to five feet of water to start up again. The average depth of the river was five to eight feet, but in some places it was less than two feet.

"Because of these conditions," River explained, "I can't always stop to look at something of interest in shallow water because we won't be able to start up again. I'm not sure what we'll see today, but there is a definite possibility of seeing eagles, bears, moose, and beaver.

"Notice that the water is moving quite fast, actually eight to 12 mph, but in the canyon it will be moving significantly faster."

River knew that in order to maintain an upstream bank speed of 30 mph, the boat had to maintain a water speed of 40 mph. This was due to the effect of the downriver current speed on the hull, similar to a headwind on an aircraft.

"Any questions?"

One lady asked, "What about logs in the river?"

"Good question!" River loved to engage his clients, especially about one of his favorite subjects. "Don't worry, we can jump over logs."

Everyone laughed, not sure if he was serious.

"Kelly Marshall is our naturalist guide today. She is going to do a little safety talk required by the Coast Guard."

Kelly began, "Hi everyone. You did sign up for the overnight trip, right?" Everyone laughed again, and Kelly completed the safety presentation.

"Thanks, Kelly," River said and then introduced Sharon. "This is Sharon Mahay, head of marketing, and she will tell you about the great trip you are about to experience today."

Sharon began, "Today we are taking a 130-mile trip, to introduce a new tour we will be adding next summer. It features a visit to Devils Canyon, an amazing area of Class V and VI whitewater. We will actually take the boat up into the canyon so you can experience the might of the longest, roughest stretch of whitewater in North America. Only a handful of people have ever ventured as far as you are going today."

River, remembering Don's warning about a slander campaign that Chet Bastian was rumored to be preparing to launch, added, "Due to modern technology that has been developed in this vessel, we can safely travel into these treacherous waters. Rest assured you will always be safe."

Sharon continued, "That's right, and on the way there, we will stop at our Indian encampment which also has an authentic trapper's cabin. We walk you through the life of a Susitna River trapper at the turn of the century. Trapping methods, fur displays, traps, cooking utensils, and so forth are exhibited for your examination. River Mahay trapped this region in the 1970s and because of his expertise, we are fortunate to have first-hand experience with the methods used by trappers."

In order to ensure that they presented an accurate display of true native life, River and his employees conducted extensive research at the Anchorage Museum of History and Art and the Alaska Native Heritage Center. Valuable information was taken from the informative book, *Shem Pete's Alaska: The Territory of the Upper Cook Inlet Dena'ina*, by James Kari and James A. Fall, and finally from the 1896 journals of William Dickey, an explorer who kept accurate journals on his discovery of the Dena'ina people.

Shem Pete was a local Dena'ina elder who lived in the area and had knowledge of the history and people that was so vast, it had been said that his knowledge was comparable to the information found in an encyclopedia.

"After leaving the Indian encampment and trapper's cabin, we will travel 20 miles farther upriver to the historic town of Curry, where we will have lunch. As an interesting side note, the Alaska Railroad is currently working with Mahay's to develop the reopening of Curry for future touring adventures.

"While we dine, you will be entertained by a video shown on the Discovery Channel of River's historic first-ever successful navigation of the mighty Devils Canyon. You will later experience the journey for yourself as River will take us into the canyon as far as we can safely go. We know you are going to love it."

Sharon nodded to River and he added, "We are not going to keep you seated for long, and promise this to be a most amazing adventure which will not soon be forgotten. After we are underway, you are welcome to walk out onto the back deck to see and feel a 1,000-horsepower engine moving water through jet units pushing a 25-ton boat 50 mph. There may be quite a bit of spray and mist. Please feel free to make yourselves comfortable."

River further added, "There is no telling what incredible wildlife we might see, so I want you all to watch closely. We are going into an area that has the highest population of black bear in Alaska and a fair number of grizzly bears. Keep close watch. Okay, everyone, time to buckle up.

"As we leave the dock, we will be on the Talkeetna River, then on to the Susitna River, and finally the 65 miles up to Devils Canyon. We will also take in the awe-inspiring view of majestic Mount McKinley and the Alaska Range spanning the entire horizon. No other view of the entire range is more spectacular than this, as long as the mountain is clear of clouds. Kelly will explain now what else you will be seeing."

Kelly described some of the sights. "Eagles are always a big part of every trip. We discovered by survey that about 50 percent of the people who take tours with us have never seen a bald eagle in its natural habitat. We will soon see a large eagle's nest that has been a landmark for 30 years. Hopefully, we'll see eagles. Watch along the tree line for beavers and the shoreline for bears.

"As Sharon pointed out earlier, this trip is dedicated to getting into Devils Canyon, which is a wild river park. We also will be going through a part of Denali State Park that is seldom visited. River is going to get underway now and put some miles behind us. Please watch for wildlife as we go. Beverages will be served along the way, and we will help you with whatever you need."

It wasn't long before they stopped at the Indian encampment and River explained, tongue-in-cheek, some of the details of the tour, which might be of concern.

"You will notice all our guides carry guns. There is a reason for this. We have left the region of the river pirates, and are now entering the region of the bears. You will see their tracks. They are real. We didn't place them here for your entertainment.

"Besides bear tracks, we might also see moose tracks. Most people are not familiar with either of these. If we have a bear encounter on the trail, we want everybody to be very quiet and still. That means no shouting, running away or screaming. A shotgun-carrying guide will get between you and the bear and everyone will start walking slowly back to the boat. At that time, we will skip this portion of the tour, and continue upriver."

The passengers stared at River, trying to decide whether or not he was serious. Sharon rolled her eyes and they all laughed.

River continued, "If all goes well, you will take a short walk along a nature trail with Kelly guiding you, to give you a chance to see some things up close and indigenous to this area."

Kelly, Sandi and Sharon helped the guests off the boat and up the ramp to the nature trail, while River tended to the boat.

The tour began immediately as Kelly pointed out some of the local plants. "This is the cow parsnip plant, from the hogweed family. These plants are found in abundance throughout this area. It is an important and valuable food for grizzly and black bears. Since it composes 33 percent of their early-summer diets and six percent of fall diets, it is no wonder we have so many bears in this area."

Kelly guided everyone through each one of the displays. "The first thing River would build whenever he started a new cabin was a food cache. It was used to store the food of the prospector, homesteader, or trapper and keep it safe from scavenging animals.

"This trapper's cabin is a true replica of the ones that River Mahay and other trappers built in the wild. Please feel free to examine the pelts. They belong to the different types of animals he trapped. You may also enter the cabin to see the items used for wilderness living.

"River built this cabin in 1994. The sod roof base is made from the bark of the birch tree. The bark is used as shingles to seal and prevent the roof from leaking and needs to be replaced about every 10 years."

"You need to get up there and mow that roof," Kitty Owens said.

Everyone laughed and Kelly agreed, "It does look like it needs mowing, but the plants up there are necessary to form root systems to hold the sod in place. Notice there are even cranberries and raspberries on the roof."

Everyone enjoyed the hands-on experience of the encampment. On the back of the cabin hung a two-man crosscut saw that had been donated to River by Herb and Bill Thompson. The brothers had used the saw when they worked on the Alaska Highway at Burwash Landing in the Yukon Territory in 1942.

"These displays are amazing," one of the clients remarked. "Does River Mahay captain all these tours?"

"He does do quite a few, but we have four captains and one of them is his son, Israel."

Kelly led them back to the boat, and everyone took their seats.

Sharon noticed that River had that worried crease in the middle of his forehead again. She leaned over out of earshot and asked, "What's up?"

"I'll tell you later," he responded. He didn't think she was ready to hear he had just had another bear encounter. It was just a black bear, but pretty large. It had come out of the woods and begun chewing on the dock, eyeballing River with a mean glare.

River was getting ready to shoot him if necessary, knowing everyone would be back any minute, but didn't want to frighten the crowd, especially since this group would decide if others should come.

The bear became startled when it heard the laughter and talk from the returning group, and sneaked off into the brush. No one except River had even seen it.

*What's going on?* he thought. Bears seemed to be coming out of the woodwork lately. He wanted to make sure Sharon loved being here with him, and the bears' untimely appearances were not helping.

## Chapter Sixteen
# Deadhorse Dinner Theater

Everyone returned to the boat and was comfortably seated when they pulled away from the dock and headed for the next part of the tour. River offered words of encouragement regarding the wildlife.

"Although we haven't seen a bear yet, don't be surprised. They are probably watching us."

Sharon shivered and scanned the shoreline looking to see if The Big One was following them. River was also scrutinizing the land for any bears, glad to be on the water where he could more easily see them. He knew seeing a bear could be the most exciting part of the trip and no one ever tired of seeing the animals, except perhaps Sharon.

He said, "We are now heading for the deserted town site of Deadhorse, later named Curry, an historic site and stopover for the Alaska Railroad."

Curry had been a halfway point for the steam engine trains traveling from Seward to Fairbanks, and they always stopped there for the night. Later, the diesel engines that could travel faster were able to make the trip in one day. This eliminated the need for a night's layover in Curry.

Curry at that time had been larger than Talkeetna, and boasted a four-star resort hotel, which was considered to be one of the finest north of Seattle. It had 105 rooms, 30 of them used for housing railroad workers and troops. The cost was $46 a night, a high price in those days.

The Curry Hotel was completed in 1923 along with the railroad. On April 9, 1957, it burned to the ground in a few hours, taking the lives of two small children and one woman. The only things saved were some cash and records. The book, *Lavish Silence*, fully depicts the history of Curry.

The cause of the fire had never been discovered. Even before the fire, the railroad had planned to abolish Curry as a stopover/maintenance depot because of increased activity in the Talkeetna area. So, all the reasons for maintaining Curry were gone, along with its grand hotel.

While Curry was in its heyday, everyone traveling to interior Alaska spent one night at the site. In the winter, there was skiing with one rope tow. Summers offered guests a small golf course and swimming pool. The town generated its own power off Deadhorse Stream.

River said, "After the fire, the Alaska Railroad came in with a bulldozer and cleared out everything. There is nothing left, except what we are about to see, which is an old boiler salvaged from a damaged locomotive, along with our own temporary picnic tables and chairs under a gazebo.

"Before the Curry Hotel was built, Curry featured a famous old building, called Deadhorse Road House. The proprietor was the famous Alaska Nellie, who was known for her incredible cooking abilities and extraordinary hunting skills. It is said that she killed the largest grizzly bear ever seen at that time."

Sharon perked up, and wished Alaska Nellie was still around to take out The Big One. She wondered, *could Nellie's bear and Big Bear be related?*

The riverboat stopped on the shore and the boarding ladders were lowered so the passengers could disembark easily. Tables with enough chairs to accommodate everyone were already set up for their dining pleasure. Sharon had hung a banner over the picnic area that read, "Deadhorse Dinner Theater." The ambiance was in place.

They carried large coolers to the tables, which contained the boxed lunches made by Mahay's own chef. Sharon and the guests made their way to the chairs, and everyone found a place to be seated.

She launched into the presentation by introducing the canyon-run video, hoping to build the excitement of what they were about to see and experience when they entered the dangerous waters of Devils Canyon.

"Just the name of it is formidable and demands respect and caution," she said. "Devils Canyon is known for its massive whitewater and has never been successfully navigated by powerboat until September 24, 1985, by River Mahay. People had died trying to navigate the treacherous waters, and the ones who lived vowed never to go again. It has Class VI rapids, which are considered unnavigable, and there is no Class VII. The movie you are about to see is real and the names have not been changed to protect the innocent. The man in the boat—making history—is none other than our very own captain."

She paused for a moment. Everyone was still and reflective. The idea was working well, and she hoped the TV-VCR would actually turn on. Kelly was preparing to start the generator.

Sharon forged on. "This movie was taped by a crew out of Anchorage. The owner of the company, Evan Swensen, told the crew they were there to record the attempt, and not to participate in a rescue if anything went wrong. Evan was well aware that there was a good chance they would be filming the death of River Mahay."

Another pause, and she continued. "This is the same movie some of you may have already seen on Alaska television stations or the Discovery Channel, who bought the rights and aired it several times a month nationally and internationally. Although the royalties never amounted to monetary gain, the exposure brought recognition."

Several people nodded and whispered to each other that they thought they remembered seeing it before.

Sharon continued. "River Mahay wanted to do something significant that had never before been accomplished. Devils Canyon had never been navigated by a jetboat. It is 12 miles of notorious Class VI whitewater on the Susitna River and considered the roughest in North America. Some men had tried it about three years prior, and ended up in the frigid waters. They survived, but lost their boat.

"The film you are about to see was shot from a helicopter, and anything shot from the air will take the water and flatten it, therefore it will not portray the full effect of what you will experience for yourself when we travel there today. Before making the actual attempt, River had flown with the helicopter pilot to get an idea of what he was facing."

Sharon finally heard the generator start up, and held her breath, waiting to see if the picture would turn on. In seconds the narrator's image appeared.

"Whew," she breathed a sigh of relief as it started, then glanced at River in the back of the crowd giving her the thumbs-up sign. She smiled, and hoped Deadhorse and Curry would once again become a booming town someday.

(left) *The Talkeetna Queen is a 55-passenger boat with Mt. McKinley in full view in the background.*

(center) *Sharon Mahay describing the trip to Tammy Bruce, Marketing Director of Mat-Su Valley Convention and Visitor's Bureau, on a Devils Canyon familiarization trip.*

(below) *For their adventure-excursion guests, Mahay's Riverboat Service makes delicious, fresh lunches.*

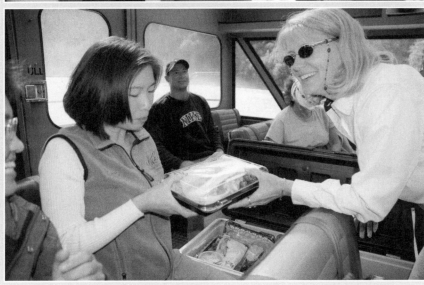

(left) River Mahay entertaining the guests and crew with his tales of wilderness adventures.

(above) River constantly checks out the shoreline for possible wildlife.

Finally, two grizzlies walking along the Susitna River shoreline. This is always a treat for the clients as well as Steve.

*(above)* The tour stops at the entrance of an abandoned beaver's lodge on the Susitna River.

*(center)* An eagle's nest, watched for many years, was finally felled in 2006 by beavers at the confluence of the Susitna and Chulitna rivers.

*(bottom)* A close-up of an eagle watching the boat, along the Susitna River.

*One of the many moose seen from the tour boat.*

*Loading up to head out for a fun day of wilderness adventure.*

*Heading toward the Indian Encampment replica, and experiencing Devils Canyon.*

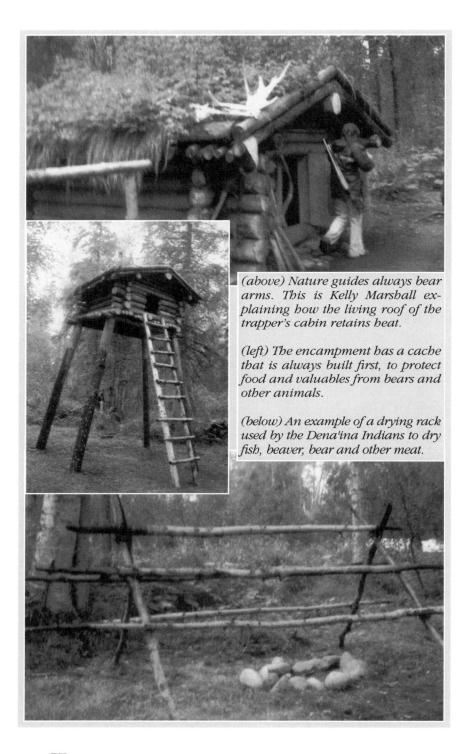

*(above) Nature guides always bear arms. This is Kelly Marshall explaining how the living roof of the trapper's cabin retains heat.*

*(left) The encampment has a cache that is always built first, to protect food and valuables from bears and other animals.*

*(below) An example of a drying rack used by the Dena'ina Indians to dry fish, beaver, bear and other meat.*

*The building of a trapper's cabin replica.*

*The trapper's cabin roof, as it was being completed.*

*This trapper's cabin, built in 1998, is a replica used for demonstration at the Susitna River Encampment, and is near the original trapper's cabin.*

*The type of cabin Steve Mahay built and used for traplines and homesteading.*

*This is the inside of the trapper's cabin, showing the types of items necessary for survival and successful trapping.*

*In 2005, River Mahay explains to clients how he used the trapper cabins and traplines.*

*(above) Animal pelts for examination.*

*(left) River Mahay showing and offering the clients an opportunity to handle a black bear pelt.*

*(below) These are pelts similar to what River Mahay harvested from the wilderness.*

*The Indian lodge, showing how a fire is built in front, while the back remains protected from the weather and animals.*

*A full view of the encampment cache, trapper's cabin and camp.*

*(above) The Dena'ina Indians used ground-based, food-storage holes like this to keep meat and salmon cool.*

*(below) Leaving the encampment to proceed to Devils Canyon.*

*(top) Captain Mahay scopes out the best course to navigate into Devils Canyon. He carefully chooses his path, using all the skill and knowledge obtained during his 1985 run.*

*(center) Devils Canyon water is getting rough. Excitement rises with the water.*

*(bottom) The tourists are quiet and mesmerized by the power and sound of the water in Devils Canyon.*

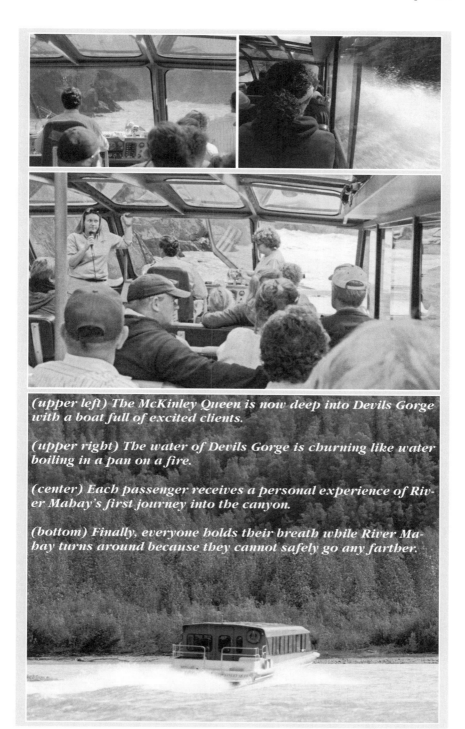

*(upper left) The McKinley Queen is now deep into Devils Gorge with a boat full of excited clients.*

*(upper right) The water of Devils Gorge is churning like water boiling in a pan on a fire.*

*(center) Each passenger receives a personal experience of River Mahay's first journey into the canyon.*

*(bottom) Finally, everyone holds their breath while River Mahay turns around because they cannot safely go any farther.*

# Chapter Seventeen
# Near-Death Revisited

The video began and she sat down to enjoy the show with the rest of the crowd.

"I don't think he is going to make it," said several local residents interviewed by Swensen's publishing company.

"A German kayaker was swept to his death while trying to ride down the canyon."

Individuals on the video spoke about a previous attempt by a group who tried to run the canyon three years prior to River. They had capsized in dangerous waters.

Sharon stopped the video and interjected, "The captain on this other trip was Glen Wooldridge, along with news reporter Steve McDonald of Anchorage as one of the crew. McDonald states to this day that he never wants to go back. He claims he is lucky to be alive. They did not find any trace of the boat. River was the medic, and had said it was a miracle any of them lived.

"What happened was the bow went down first, filled up with water and then sank. Before their attempt, River expressed his concern. They had told him what they were going to do, and the boat they planned on using was more of a race boat. He had waved goodbye to them and his concerns increased when they came back 10 minutes later and asked for directions, as well as for five-gallon buckets for bailing, just in case they took on water."

Sharon continued. "River said if you don't go in there with the type of mindset to make it or sink the boat, you'll turn around because you are too scared. The boat in which River chose to do the run is named *Kristine*. It is still operational and is used every day by Mahay's Riverboat Service. Although the canyon was frightening, there was something novel about trying to do something no one else had ever done before."

Sharon resumed playing the video and they listened to Vern Rockenstein, owner of the Swiss Alaska Inn, try to talk River out of doing the run. Many people in the community depended on him.

River had been listening to the video and thought about the details of that day when he had risked everything, including his life. Fate had been looking out for him, and he'd been well prepared. Don Lee had flown him up several times to check out the dangers and look for obstacles. *We really did our homework for this run, and it paid off,* he thought.

Four days before the scheduled attempt, rain fell and the river rose. In Devils Canyon, high water means severe rapids. Some waves reach 15 to 20 feet. Success required the right water flow rate, but too much could be disastrous also. He'd postponed the run a year earlier because of high water.

The boat he had used was a 27-foot vessel that could hit a boulder and almost kill everyone on board, but still keep going. It was a tank. Everything not necessary for the ride had been taken off the boat. No extra fuel weight. A helicopter had airlifted extra fuel over the canyon to resupply the boat for the remaining 150-mile river trip after the rapids, which would take them up the Susitna River to the bridge near the Denali Highway.

River used Styrofoam in the boat to ensure it would continue to float if capsized. The cockpit was rigged to allow an easy escape if the boat sank. Two plywood shields placed over the existing windows provided additional reinforcement. He'd had his windshields blown out before by the water pressure, filling the boat with hundreds of gallons of water in seconds. He didn't want this to happen here, because it was not just a matter of calling it quits and floating downstream for repairs. The video commentator continued:

> There is a moment before any noble quest where stark reality sets in. If he was successful, people would view him as a hero, but if he failed, what then? Some men look forward to some event or challenge, but when it happens, it seems too soon. Mount McKinley will be watching to see how its cousin of the valley, the Susitna, will fare.
>
> Four days of rain took place, the weather broke, and the water subsided. He and friends prayed for his safety. One last helicopter trip was made to check out the river, because the next time he faced it, he would be in its grip. There were two cameras on the trip, most of the way.

River returned to his memories of that day. There were four dangerous spots in the canyon. This group would actually experience a portion of the first one, called Devils Gorge. River had gone much farther into the gorge, which not only had steep walls and 12-foot standing waves but was the narrowest spot in the canyon. This section was bad enough....but it got worse.

There were three other dangerous spots called Hotel Rock, the Nozzle, and finally the Boiling Pot. Just the names alone were enough to keep a conservative person from ever wanting to go near them. But River never considered himself a conservative person.

Before running each difficult rapid, River had flown in the helicopter and tried to memorize the best course to maneuver the boat through the trouble spots. He had a coldwater rescue team in place with a cargo net that could be lowered into the water to rescue him. They flew over the boat as it ascended the rapids. Don Lee was flying overhead in a Cessna fixed-wing aircraft at a high-enough altitude to provide radio contact with the outside world if needed. River had been anxious to get underway after years of preparation for this dangerous and historic attempt.

River's first encounter with the dangers of a 90-degree turn while going through 15-to 20-foot waves had almost ended in disaster. In less than 20 yards, he had to pilot the boat on a narrow backwater eddy.

He then had to jump the boat out of the eddy and into raging water that put him directly perpendicular to the line of travel of his vessel. This caused a huge blast of water against the starboard side that threatened to sweep him sideways into the canyon wall.

In order to align himself properly in the river flow, he had to turn the boat 90 degrees within a few short yards, or be smashed into the downstream canyon wall, making for a very short trip. This location was the spot where Glen Wooldridge and his party had sunk their boat three years before. No boat had ever gone past this point.

The video showed River as he had powered up the small eddy line and jumped into the powerful flow of water. He remembered that he had to use maximum power while holding a full starboard turn.

River realized he was not going to make the turn and was about to be slammed into the canyon wall at a 45-degree angle. He eased off the power a half second before hitting the wall because he needed to make as sharp a turn as possible in the fast-flowing current before impacting the wall.

The river slammed him against the canyon wall as hard as if his boat had been dropped from an office building. The impact propelled him head first into the windshield before bouncing him onto the boat's floor. The boat shuddered from the current as the canyon wall hammered it into submission. He jumped up and regained control before realizing he had broken off three front teeth. Spitting them out, he saw where his teeth had left dents on the aluminum window frame. River could hear the specter of defeat laughing at him like a cruel heckler. He heard its taunts and felt its discouragement. River thought, *the river should have killed me right there.* He ignored the voices, focused, and quickly reviewed the situation.

He took control with confidence. The force had bounced the boat in such a manner that it had aligned him perfectly with the flow of the water. He had successfully made the 90-degree turn—the first 45 degrees was by the power of the boat, and the second, by the impact of the wall—with a perfect combination of skill and luck.

The impact killed the power, and he had expected short circuits, but all systems remained operational. The current now sucked him into the base of a standing wave that was larger than his cabin. He maneuvered the boat, swimming it like a salmon in the bottom of a whitewater trough. Suddenly he spotted an opening, headed for it at full throttle, and was awestruck that it worked and he was still alive.

*No one in the world had ever been in water like this.* It was a combination of luck, cunning, and good old-fashioned horsepower that got him through. He was in a state of bewilderment, a semi-awareness. He didn't remember how the bow did not get wet. He was alive, although again subdued in spirit. He had just started his run and already had huge difficulties. From this point on, there was no turning back.

Looking upriver, he breathed heavily. His arms vibrated in challenged trepidation. What he just endured wasn't even the worst. This realization prepared his mindset and steeled his resolve. He focused on the water at the bow. Perhaps it was better that he didn't know what was coming.

There was one other spot that was worse than the first, but after the initial obstacle had been overcome, River had taken some recovery time. It was at this point that he faced the obvious truth: He had only a slim chance of completing the run, or coming through it alive.

Aware of the importance of maintaining concentration and avoid becoming too fearful, he remembered how he had trained to become one with the boat, knowing he had the skill to maneuver the boat with a precision of inches.

Just before running the next two major rapids, the Nozzle and the Boiling Pot, all three cameras had run out of film, and there is no film footage of the most dangerous parts of the canyon for anyone to see.

This had been unfortunate, since all cameras had been placed in opportune positions, one on the shore, one mounted on the helicopter directly overhead, and the third handheld in the helicopter. It could have been a great Kodak moment.

In the very bowels of the canyon, the water was roaring and slamming into walls at 30 mph. River had to pick and choose where he needed to go, and then sneak through the rest. He studied the next segment, a titan of whitewater-churning chaos with a deafening roar that shook the boat with its raw power. For several minutes he tried to find a clear route around the boulders and rapids, to no avail. He had a fleeting thought about calling for the helicopter to pick him up right there and let the boat go. He was at his wit's end. The whitewater seemed impossible to run, *and* suicidal. Again, he felt fear bite him like a rattlesnake, feeling the poison of its discouragement course through his veins. Yet, he had not come this far to call it quits. The only way to conquer this canyon was to continue until he either made it or lose the boat trying. There was no turning back. Again he bolstered himself and looked for solutions rather than excuses for quitting. It is what legends do when they feel they can't go on anymore. They get up and go, despite the outcome.

River had spotted a 20-yard eddy behind a massive, upstream boulder. He maneuvered the boat into the current and held his position, studying the turbulent chaos in front of him. He hovered above a 15-to 20-foot vertical drop, which resembled a giant open mouth, ready to swallow his boat into the cold numbness of the river, never to be seen again. The worst possible route was the only one available to River.

River peered at a diagonal V at one place in the vertical drop, and saw an opening to possibly climb up out of this whitewater maw. If he didn't move diagonally with the V, the river would sweep him back and defeat him. He had no idea if he could make it, and realistically believed he could not. It was his only opportunity. He had to try.

He maneuvered the boat onto the lower part of the V. The engines roared as he throttled to maximum power. He inched his way into the current while moving diagonally across the face of the vertical drop. If he stayed in the V, it would not be a 90-degree vertical drop but a 45-degree incline. The boat had just enough thrust at maximum to move slowly up this 45-degree incline. It was like walking a tightrope in a hurricane. Staying in the V taxed him beyond anything he had encountered so far. One slip, one edge caught in the current, and the boat would capsize.

River's knowledge of his vessel and experience on the river paid off, and he maintained control until he crested the vertical drop. The currents mellowed, the canyon loosened its deathly grip and conceded defeat. River entered the upper canyon site and had overcome his last obstacle. He had done it!

River secured the boat at a safe anchoring site on shore, and celebrated with the support crew, having achieved what had been the unachievable. His teeth hurt badly, but he was glad to be alive. He had done it, but would never do it again. Fate had saved his life, but he knew better than to push it. The event had made the front page of the *Anchorage Daily News*.

River's brother, Joe Mahay, and one of River's friends had joined him for the rest of the trip. They were part of the support crew flown in by helicopter, and they remained with him for the next two days. They traveled 150 miles farther upriver to the area where the Susitna River and Denali Highway meet. There was no other exit route.

They camped out on the tundra near a bluff overlooking the Susitna River Valley. It seemed they were able to see forever, as if they had stepped back in time. There were moose, caribou, grizzly and black bears feeding on the mountain slopes. There were no signs of humans ever being there, only animals.

The water and air temperature had dropped fast over the last two days, and the river channels were disappearing. If they didn't get the boat out soon, it would be hopelessly stuck there for the winter.

River used a radio to contact the Gracious House Lodge on the Denali Highway, but failed to connect. They were on their own. After traveling all day, they finally made it to the bridge. River's entire trip had ended up being more than 210 miles.

The video was giving its grand finale.

One more piece of Alaska's vanishing wilderness had been captured. River Mahay turned a dream into reality. The river he conquered remains unchanged, but the man will never be the same. He took a chance and realized his dream. Many people experience the breathtaking beauty of Alaska, but few accept her calling or challenge. The water was a force of nature, but when you are living on the edge, there's no time to worry about tomorrow.

Alaska was a good teacher, with hard lessons, but worth the effort. Problem is, not everyone passes the tests.

*River standing on the bow of one of his boats on the Susitna River, looking at Mt. McKinley and the Alaska Range.*

*River Mahay is at the helm and turning off the Talkeetna River onto the Susitna River.*

*River Mahay and crew preparing to leave dock and begin his historic Devils Canyon run.*

(upper left) Historic landmark made by explorer William Dickey, carved into the rock in 1897 near the entrance of Devils Canyon.

(upper right) Steve Mahay in safety gear before he runs Devils Canyon.

(lower) Support group reviewing a cargo net and life ring rescue devices to retrieve Steve Mahay in the event of his boat sinking in the massive waves of Devils Canyon.

*Steve Mahay discussing his strategy with TV film crew prior to running Devils Canyon.*

*Support crew waiting to hear word via helicopter radio or airplane spotter that Steve Mahay made it safely through the canyon.*

*(upper) A view of Devils Canyon from the observation and rescue heli-copter. (lower) River Mahay taking a breather between stretches of Devils Canyon whitewater to choose the best possible route.*

River Mahay caught in a wave that slammed him into the wall on his famous Devils Canyon run. He quickly recovered and sped out of the canyon, and into the history books.

Upon successfully completing the run, Steve Mahay found a piece of the rock cliff he slammed into embedded in the side of his boat.

**Steve Mahay survives treacherous Devils Canyon Wednesday as a helicopter film crew records the event**

# Jet boater survives Devils Canyon

by Bill Sherwonit
Times Outdoors Writer

His boat was battered against massive rock walls, swallowed up by foaming, frothing 15-foot waves and at times tossed completely out of water. But Steve Mahay did Wednesday what no man or woman had done before: he took his 27-foot inboard jet boat up the Susitna River, through Devils Canyon.

Mahay had to pass through some of the most treacherous whitewater on the North America continent to become the first person to pilot a powerboat through the world-famous canyon, located about 50 miles northeast of Talkeetna.

"It was no easy deal," said Talkeetna Air Taxi owner Don Lee, who flew above the canyon while videotaping Mahay's historic riverboat ride. "I was pretty worried most of the time he was in the canyon. There were a couple times when he was completely out of control, that I didn't think he'd make it. But Steve did the job. He knew exactly what he was doing."

Mahay, a professional guide and river-runner, is scheduled to arrive back in Talkeetna today. After completing his 12-mile "mission impossible" late Wednesday afternoon, the 38-year-old owner of Mahay's Riverboat Service continued upriver to Susitna Landing rather than try a return run through Devils Canyon.

"It would have been crazy to try and bring the boat downstream through those rapids," explained Lee, who helped to sponsor the attempt. "So when he got through the canyon, Steve refueled the boat and headed for Susitna Landing, where he'll take the boat out and haul it back to Talkeetna."

To complete his trip, Mahay had to pilot his boat through four major sets of rapids. In places, the waters of the Susitna were squeezed between canyon walls only 20 feet apart. The waves that were created stood as high as 15 feet.

Lee, who watched the whole show from the air, said, "The boat hit the canyon walls several times. Sometimes the boat was completely out of the water — literally up on the rocks — and at other times it was totally submerged. He'd hit a wall of water and just disappear into that white foam, then appear again. He just kept smashing into huge waves. You just couldn't believe it."

The last and perhaps toughest obstacle was the last set of rapids, known as Hotel Rock. There, the Su-
See Research, page A-14

*The* Anchorage Times *article the day after Steve's Devils Canyon run. Local TV stations also covered the event during their evening news broadcasts.*

*Steve Mahay powering through the last stretch of rapids in Devils Canyon.*

## Chapter Eighteen
# Devils Canyon: A Whitewater Hell

The tour group completed lunch as video credits flashed on the screen and the amazing video presentation came to a close. The anticipation from watching River's experience made them eager to continue. Sharon's arrangement was a smashing success. Everyone felt they had personally made the historic run with River Mahay. They were excited to enter Devils Canyon. They walked a fast pace back to the boat and took their seats. River fired up the engines, and they were soon on their way. The boat's jet pumps roared to power, and sped the group to its appointment with whitewater destiny.

Before entering the canyon, River paused the boat so everyone could take pictures. The sound alone created feelings of being caught in a massive whitewater tornado. No one but River had ever heard anything like it before. Some compared it to standing inside a giant waterfall.

"Okay," River said, "Everyone take your seats. We are now entering Devils Canyon. I'm going to put the microphone down because things might get a little busy from here on in."

Hearts pounded with excitement as the boat entered the section where River began his famous whitewater run. He took the boat into the beginning of Devils Gorge, just below the rapids where Glen Wooldridge sank his boat. The roar of the waves vibrated the boat with the power of an earthquake. The churning river kicked up a 10-foot haystack that River skillfully maneuvered.

Sharon looked around. People were transfixed with the sight, and a few seemed to hold their breath. They were reliving what each considered was the feeling that River Mahay must have had when he ran the canyon in 1985. Holding the boat in the rapids, the roar of the water was so loud that his passengers could barely hear River as he shouted, "It's pretty incredible when we get in there. The water level is low today, but we'll see how far we can safely go."

The sound was becoming deafening as River took the boat even farther into the gorge. He said, "This is the point of no return. We are in Devils Gorge, which is the smallest and most dangerous spot of the canyon. See where it narrows up ahead? Another jetboater, by the name of Daryl Bentz, who was also the builder and designer of this boat, successfully ran Devils Canyon in 2000, with a boat similar in style to the jetboat I used. He is the only other person to have done it to this date.

"Okay, you can move around shortly, while I hold the boat here. This is as far as we can go. Take a look up front. It looks pretty nasty. Each time you come in here it will be different. I'm farther up than I usually go because the water level is lower than usual. You can take pictures now."

"Oh my gosh, look … it's absolutely beautiful." Each guest was mesmerized by the treacherous yet spellbinding surroundings.

"I lost my teeth up around that corner and could not turn back. I think we can make it up a little farther, if you like," River said.

No one was saying anything. Some brave souls wanted to agree, but most wanted to say, "No, turn back!"

"You can get up on the bow if you want and take pictures."

No one moved, and one lady asked Sharon, "He's not serious, is he?"

Sharon shrugged her shoulders and said, "He wouldn't think twice about going out there to take pictures, but I wouldn't go."

River heard Sharon's comment and said, "I can't figure out why the people who know me the best trust me the least."

Everyone laughed, relieving tension.

Suddenly, River called out, "Hang on, it's getting rough. There's a boulder over there on the left—it could open up this boat like a tin can. This is some of the roughest whitewater in the world, and considered unnavigable. Shall we turn around? Or do you want to continue?"

He couldn't hear the answers over the raging roar of the water churning over the boulders, but shouted, "Hold on to your personal possessions!"

Everyone was captivated as he turned the boat around and headed back down the river a short distance to escape the deafening roar of the terrifying, cascading turbulence emanating from Devils Gorge.

There were no words to describe what they had just seen and experienced, so no one said anything. Each was in a personal world of thoughts about the feel of the massive power of Devils Canyon.

River's own thoughts were that he would never put his life on the line again, as he had for that run. He was glad he had done it, but relieved it was over.

*How did he survive*, some wondered.

Another said, "That was the most incredible trip I have ever completed. I thought it was going to be more frightening, but it was invigorating."

The people on board were feeling exhilarated from having partici- pated in something very few people had ever experienced, yet at the same time realized this was something their grandparents or small children would enjoy, and never forget.

After heading downriver a short distance, River pulled into Portage Creek for a break and to observe the spawning salmon. The water was clear and calm, which allowed the passengers to watch those beauti- ful, large salmon make their final journey to the spawning grounds.

River pointed in the direction of a rock outcropping and said, "Notice the names chipped into the rock by four early explorers. Remember when we previously discussed William Dickey, the first explorer to make it this far up? He actually carved his name and the date into that rock."

River remembered how he had brought some tourists to this spot once, and they went on foot, scouting the area. One lady had de- cided to take a break and read a book, while sitting on the rock. She suddenly called out to him, 'Have you ever seen this before?' She was pointing at the carving and River had not known it was there.

He said, "On that rock base, right over there, is Dickey's name carved along with three other guys, along with the date of July 2, 1897. They stood right there on the beach, had their own canoe and documented the Dena'inas. If you have binoculars, you might be able to see it."

On the Indian River, 15 miles downstream from Portage, they stopped and again viewed the spawning salmon. Around 1910, a roadhouse had been built there, and served as an early route into the Interior be- fore the railroad was constructed. They came on the water by barge, or paddle wheeler and hiked along Indian River to and through Broad Pass, then into the Interior. It was a little-known route.

River had hiked a great deal in the area, and had never found any traces of the roadhouse, but he was sure the remains were out there, somewhere.

They proceeded downriver another three miles to the Alaska Rail- road Susitna River Bridge. River said, "This is the Gold Creek Rail- road Bridge, built in 1921. There used to be a maintenance station here. This small community received its name from the gold found in the creek."

In the late 1920s and early 1930s, there had been around 300 people who made their wages with shovels and wooden rockers by digging along the beach. They panned for gold along the length of the banks. The area had been commercially mined up until about 15 years ago, when a dredge went through the creek and took most of the gold.

People were still captivated by the experience of Devils Canyon, and had little to say, but someone asked, "When are we going to see a grizzly bear?"

Sharon looked quickly toward the person with the question, and thought, *Never, I hope.*

River said, "We're going to see a grizzly bear soon. I'm real confident. You never know what might be in the woods and there very well might be a bear feeding close by."

Sharon fought off the chills that ran down her spine.

River felt a little uneasy too. He had spotted a bear a couple of times, watching the boat, and wondered if it had been The Big One. It seemed to be following their voyage. Suddenly, one of the guests shouted, "There's a bear!"

Everyone immediately glanced in the direction he was pointing, and there he was, The Big One, on a ledge overlooking the river, studying the boat and its passengers as if they were the ones in a cage at the zoo.

The people were thrilled to have seen a bear and Sharon felt sick. *It did seem like he was always nearby,* she thought.

# Chapter Nineteen
# River Runs

So far the day had been a great success. Nothing had gone wrong, and the bear spotting was almost as exciting to the clients as going into the canyon. Everyone loved this new Devils Canyon tour. The excitement that built from showing the video had worked perfectly, and turned out to be exactly what Sharon and River had hoped for. The clients loved it and now that they had seen the canyon firsthand, some wanted to watch the video again. Sharon explained they had extra copies back at the office. Comments were made that it was better than some of the rides in Disneyland. Sharon, River, Sandi, and Kelly were feeling pretty good.

"Hey, how'd you get that bear to show up?" asked one of the clients.

"I told you we would see a bear," answered River while avoiding Sharon's eyes.

The trip back would go much faster, because now they were going with the current, downriver. Maneuvering a boat in and out of the channels without markers is difficult, but seemed effortless with River Mahay at the helm.

"What's next, River?" Matt Conway asked. "Another river to run? What about other runs, like the Talkeetna Canyon?"

"He already did that, too," Sharon said.

"Really? When?"

"Late July, 1992," said River.

Matt asked and everyone agreed, "Can you tell us about it?"

River reached back into the recesses of his mind, wanting to give them the most accurate account. Navigating the Talkeetna River presented an entirely different set of problems than Devils Canyon. The Talkeetna River has about a quarter the volume of water of the Susitna River. This means that in the canyon, the boulders are exposed, making a severe obstacle course. River's challenge at that point had been to maneuver through the boulder fields without sustaining hull damage.

Once he recovered from the effects of running Devils Canyon, in 1985, River had wanted to run the Talkeetna River. He had been willing to gamble against the odds one more time. It wasn't out of his blood yet. No one had ever navigated more than 27 miles up the river. So, he went up 50 miles to a place called Prairie Creek, where no jetboat had ever gone. After having reached his goal of navigating the canyon and reaching Prairie Creek, he had realized it was not realistic to navigate the vessel back downstream without sustaining substantial damage and maybe sinking it. Too many boulders in too many places made any attempt exceedingly risky.

"Anyone know why you can go upriver but not down?" River quizzed the passengers.

No one knew the answer, so River explained.

"Because of the river current. You have even less control going with the flow, for the same reason planes shouldn't land with a tailwind."

"Oh, that makes sense."

"Why did you decide to run another canyon? I thought you said you had had enough," asked Patricia Kelsey.

"I did say that, but when I was over the terror of Devils Canyon, I was ready to do something else that had never been accomplished."

There was something inside of River, intrinsic to his personal nature, that caused a need to indulge in the emotional cascade and complete obsession of yet another whitewater run. He had to go the distance one more time, to prove to himself and the world that his survival and accomplishment in Devils Canyon wasn't luck or chance. If he could do this, conquer another run, to go where no one had gone before, he would then walk away a new person, wiser and more enlightened.

Now that the fear of the Devils Canyon experience was over, he discovered that the anticipation without the hope of realization created pain. When it came to the river, he was like an addict. The dopamine buzz supercharged his brain with thoughts of whitewater explorations and rituals of surviving. He wanted the buzz to continue. He was willing to return to normal and celebrate the fact that he had experienced it. But the anticipation of another whitewater run was a tonic, a spur to his soul, and he would need to deal with this painful emptiness until he could go there again.

"Because Devils Canyon had been a success, I prepared the boat basically the same way for the Talkeetna run," River said. "Everything that I needed to do to give me the best chance of achieving my goal was put back in place."

The groundwork for this run, however, had been even more thorough. Instead of just checking out the river by air, River floated the canyon with expert rafters Steve Hanson and Chad Valentine. This was the first time he had ever rafted, and afterward, he decided rafting was more dangerous than taking a boat through the rocks.

This had been a scouting trip so he could study the different stretches of rapids that were the most difficult. A major difference between the Devils Canyon and the Talkeetna Canyon was that the Devils Canyon had four difficult rapids to navigate with breaks in between, from which he had been able to rest. The actual rapids of Devils Canyon were a total of three miles long, although they were Class VI. The Talkeetna Canyon is Class IV and V, but about 14 straight miles of rapids, which would obviously be exhausting with no way of taking a break.

In 1991, he had planned to run the canyon, but low-water conditions made it extremely dangerous. Unlike the Susitna River, which needed low-water conditions, the Talkeetna River needed high-water conditions in order to cover the many boulders that he would have to avoid. Extremely low water would mean too many boulders, making it impossible to run and survive.

Fortunately in late July, there had been heavy rains in the Talkeetna Mountains. The river was near flood stage. This had been the window of opportunity that River had been looking for to make the first-ever jetboat ascent up the Talkeetna River. The preparations had been made and the time had finally come.

Since it would take 75 minutes by boat to get to the first rapids, which were 27 miles upriver, River boarded a helicopter and flew the canyon, studying the different rapids. Everything looked good. He could set a navigable course upstream, but soon realized that coming back downstream would likely be impossible.

The first rapids encountered were called Bobby Socks. He hunted and pecked his way through the boulders. His concentration was tense and the strain was to the point of making him wonder how he would ever last. Every skill he ever had was tested as his eyes strained to see where the boulders waited to claim his boat and perhaps his life. Somehow he made it through.

The next portion was called Sluice Box. It was the most dangerous part of the canyon because it was a four-mile stretch continuous with jagged boulders referred to as can openers. River couldn't see them until he was almost on top of them. If he hit one, it would slice open the boat and sink it. This was the reason that the water needed to be high enough to go over them, but to miss them all would be very difficult. It was a long stretch. By the time he got through this section, he was physically and emotionally exhausted.

Lastly, he encountered the Toilet Bowl. Kayakers considered this stretch to be most difficult because of several complicated turns and tight spots. Because of River's skills with the boat, he found the turns the easiest to negotiate.

Sharon said, "He likes to joke that this run was effortless, but does anyone believe that, after what you experienced today from the force of the river in Devils Gorge?"

"No way," said Alex Stone. "It must have been brutal."

"It actually was," River agreed. "Most of the time I was fighting to maintain control. After a certain amount of time, it wears on you because you are always bracing yourself for the hits. When you get to the worst, you slam the throttle forward and hang on. By the time I arrived at the Toilet Bowl, I was exhausted; literally wiped out."

River had thought about bringing the boat back downriver. The number of submerged boulders, plus not having as much control going downriver, all contributed to the high probability that he would lose the boat. He did not want that to happen, especially since he used the boat every day to do his real job, and had tours planned for its use. So, in order to get it back safely he had had to airlift it out. This created another dilemma because the helicopter had a hard time picking it up.

Two helicopters helped him out with this canyon run. A smaller one was used for support, as an extra pair of eyes in the sky, and was flown by a female helicopter pilot. The largest helicopter was a Sikorsky, and it would take all its power to lift his boat out of the canyon.

As the helicopter lifted the jetboat, overload stress inverted the blades beyond the normal safe condition. The pilot was about 40 feet in the air before he lost what was called the ground effect. Suddenly, the helicopter began to fall from the sky. The pilot had no other choice than to drop the boat. It landed in the river, and began drifting into the Toilet Bowl.

River's heart broke as his runaway boat drifted toward the rapids that he had just navigated. He thought about Glen Wooldridge's boat, and how they never found it. A small boulder island was the only hope that could prevent the boat from being destroyed in the rapids. To his joy, the boat struck the boulders of the upstream side of the island and hung up there. This was a rare time when he was grateful for a grounded boat, and it appeared the boat would stay put.

River climbed into the helicopter and had the pilot hover over the boat while he climbed out onto the skid and jumped to the boat below. This seemed like a fairly harmless thing to do, but the action nearly caused the demise of the whole venture, and their lives. When he jumped off the skid of the helicopter, his weight created an imbalance, and the tail rudder dipped radically downward, and for a moment, actually went into the river before the pilot could recover. They nearly crashed the helicopter into the boat, which would have killed the pilot and River. Fortunately, fate was on his side one more time.

After the crisis was over, they thanked God for their good fortune and survival. River checked out the controls and instruments of the vessel. Everything seemed to be operational. The boat was teetering on the boulder it had drifted onto, and he was able to push it free. He immediately started the engine and headed upstream to where they originally had tried to perform the airlift.

Because of this experience, they realized it would be necessary to lighten the boat even more. They removed the windows and fuel tanks, seats and equipment. The helicopter pilot now felt that he would be able to lift the boat. It needed to be carried over the 14-mile canyon and set back in the river so River could continue the 27-mile journey back to Talkeetna.

With the extra weight removed, the helicopter airlifted the boat easily and placed it in the Talkeetna River just below Iron Creek. Once in Talkeetna, River claimed another triumphant canyon run.

Getting back to the business at hand, he pulled the boat into the dock, and the clients disembarked for the bus that waited to take them back to town.

Mike was awaiting their return, and anxiously asked how it went. They were happy to report it was a complete success.

"Great!" exclaimed Mike. "Tell me all about it at dinner. See you about six?"

"Perfect," answered Sharon, and River nodded. He had forgotten their dinner date. Sharon laughed and shook her head. "I'm sorry. I guess I forgot to remind you for the 10th time."

River laughed and said, "You know how important it is to remind me at least 10 times."

On the way home, Sharon remembered hearing River talk about another run. So she asked, "Didn't you run the Cook Inlet, too?"

"I did. One day I decided to run a boat from Talkeetna to Anchorage. I had already run a boat from Talkeetna to the Denali Highway, 210 miles upstream of Talkeetna. But if I ran a boat from Talkeetna to Anchorage, then I would have completed the whole river system."

Sharon said, "I know you did those runs because no one had ever done them before, but was it worth risking your life?"

"I can say yes, now that they are done, but I don't want to risk my life unnecessarily anymore. Doing the runs gave me a great deal of personal accomplishment and the opportunity to develop my skills, and I guess if something is easy, then anyone can do it. Actually, the Talkeetna to Anchorage run had been done, just not for a long time.

They used to run large boats along this part of the river to supply the village of Talkeetna and another place called Susitna Station, which is no longer there. They ran large barges up there, but not since 80 years ago. So being the marketing person I am, I called up the Channel 2 news team and said, 'Look, I'm doing a run that hasn't been done for 80 years, and I'm going to run a boat from Talkeetna to Anchorage, down the Big Su, then go across Cook Inlet into town.'

"So they went with me to film it, and all went relatively well."

"Uh oh," Sharon mused. "Relatively well sounds like another one of your famous near-death stories."

"Well, sorta. The run took three hours and twenty minutes, which was faster than the train, but the thing I didn't calculate was the need to watch the tide. Because the Susitna River has a huge delta area that dumps into Cook Inlet, we never even looked at the tide charts. The problem became obvious when we tried to get through at low tide.

"The water all around me was disappearing and there was no place to go. Not realizing at first what was happening, I just kept trying to run ahead of the disappearing water, but eventually ran out of water and grounded out. We came to a screeching stop. The camera crew and everyone fell forward, the equipment tipped over, but, fortunately, nobody was injured. Then we had to wait for the tide to come back which takes a while."

"I can't believe it," said Sharon.

"Well, it gets worse."

"There's a surprise."

"I know. What we weren't really aware of was the bore tides that also come through there, fast. I was in a 27-foot vessel and it could have sunk our boat, but fortunately for us, that day the tide was not fast. It wasn't until afterward that I learned more about the bore tides and what they can do. I discovered just how much we were at risk."

"You just never know, do you? Things seem so innocent and then you find out something drastic is going to happen, like that." Sharon snapped her fingers and had a picture of them in her mind—sitting in the mud, waiting for the water to come back. "You were pretty fortunate, again."

"I sure was. And I'd learned a good lesson. If you ever run from Talkeetna to Anchorage with a boat, you better check the tide because you want to go through at high tide."

They laughed as easily as only two people who know each other could do.

# Chapter Twenty
# Special Friends

River and Sharon arrived at the home of Mike Stewart and his wife, Mary, two minutes early. River hated to be late, so he seldom was. It had been 24 hours since their encounter with The Big One, and by now both were once again feeling comfortable and relaxed. They enjoyed spending time with the couple, and Mary was a fantastic cook. An evening of great food and companionship was assured.

Mary had prepared a beautiful fresh salad, using vegetables from their garden, and Mike cooked moose on the grill. River loved to eat simply. Dessert was homemade apple pie, warmed and with ice cream on top, Sharon's favorite. After dinner, they went into the living room and Mike started a fire to take the chill off, because the evenings were becoming cooler, and the fire gave the room a cozy atmosphere.

Mike could hardly wait for the evening to begin and could barely contain his excitement over a surprise planned later in the evening for River and Sharon—the arrival of their dear friends Peter and Ginny Stanley—who were in town unexpectedly and would be joining the dinner party later in the evening.

They were also anxious to hear "the rest of the story" of meeting The Big One. Generally a pacifist, Mike had first come into the wilderness refusing to use a gun, but was now ready to go after The Big One right then and there.

"No, Mike," Sharon insisted. "The Big One saved my life. It was that other one, the Demon Bear, who wanted me for dinner."

"Either way," he said, "we have to do something about those bears."

"I know," agreed River, "and I haven't had a chance to tell Sharon about the bear I saw today at the Indian encampment. A black bear walked out of the woods, toward the dock, and thinking he was coming after me, I prepared to shoot him. Suddenly, he stopped and chewed on the handrail, but when he heard the crowd making its way back to the boat, he took off. I didn't think it would create a good impression to kill him in front of our tour group, but I also never got the impression that he was dangerous."

"That's why you were acting a little strange when we came back to the boat. I wish I had seen it—whoa. Did I say that?"

"Sharon, I think you are becoming a sourdough," said Mike. "Speaking of bear encounters, do you remember about two springs ago, our shoot-out on the bluff?"

"Sure do," River answered, laughing.

"I thought that bear was going to chew me up for sure," Mike said, also laughing.

"Why is that funny?" Sharon asked, shaking her head and wondering if there wasn't something wrong with people who spent winters in Alaska. They thought the oddest things were humorous.

"It wasn't funny thinking about getting chewed up," Mike said. "But there was a happy ending for us."

River began, "It was spring, mid-May, and bears were coming out on sunny sides of exposed hills to eat the newly emergent vegetation. The snow had melted off by then. Black bears coming out of hibernation are the best-eating bears. If you could get one to two for the lockers, it would get you through the summer, but this spring we were not finding too many. So, Mike and I decided to jetboat up the river, kill the engine and case both sides of the mountain. The hills were about 2,000-feet high, so we had good visibility, seeing for half a mile or more.

"Drifting near the shoreline, we eventually spotted one on a 200-foot bank. It's difficult to shoot from a drifting boat, so we secured the boat 30-feet down from the bear. Mike had a .300 Winchester Magnum and got off on the shore first, about 25 feet downstream from where the bear was sitting on the bluff, and shot him. He started rolling down the bluff, and stopped rolling at Mike's feet."

Mike added, "He was actually touching me."

River paused for effect, pleased that Sharon was leaning forward with a wide-eyed look that seemed to ask, 'What was going to happen next?'

"All of a sudden, the bear stood up."

"Oh no. I hate these stories," Sharon said, and Mary shook her head. She had obviously heard it before.

"Well, Mike was too close to get another shot on him, and I couldn't shoot for fear of hitting Mike, so I started shouting instructions, 'Take him with your handgun.' He finally drew it out and proceeded to shoot the .44 Magnum. Each time he shot, the bear jumped, and Mike jumped. He looked like he was in serious trouble."

"He who?" asked Sharon.

Mike interjected, "Me. I kept frantically shooting, and River couldn't get a clean shot for fear of hitting me. Finally, on the last round the bear went down. He had multiple wounds to all his extremities, but only one fatal shot. Frightened me half to death. I'd probably still be shooting, if I hadn't run out of bullets."

"Oh my gosh," Sharon exclaimed. "You guys are too much. Mike, I thought you didn't want to use guns."

"Yeah, well, it's pretty foolish to be in the wilderness and unable to protect your family from danger."

Sharon agreed, but wanted to give her impression of the two of them bear hunting.

"I can just see what might happen if you two went out after The Big One," she said. "If it was just Big Bear, who doesn't seem to be looking for trouble, it would probably work. But there is another ticked-off bear that is the problem. I'm afraid your shoot-out at the OK Corral could possibly turn into a Tombstone for someone other than the bears."

"I don't think we are in danger from either bear," River said. "But they have become a nuisance."

"Hey, Mike," Sharon said. "What made you change the way you felt about guns? Was it one experience, or just living in the wilderness in general?"

"Mostly, one experience in particular. We came out to Alaska about the same time as River. We were homesteading too. We were building our cabin, and unlike your 'River Boone' character, I used a chain saw."

"But no gun," River said.

"That's right. I had just returned from Vietnam and wanted nothing to do with guns. So, there we were, trying to live off the land, with a little baby, no gun, and a battery-operated chain saw. One day, while we were working on the cabin, we had our son sitting in a swing, hanging from a limb. Suddenly, a bear comes out of the woods and heads straight for the baby. I grabbed the chain saw, went after him with it and chased him off. My heart was pounding and Mary and I were trembling."

"That is horrible," Sharon said.

Mary agreed. "I was petrified. We didn't have any cabin walls up yet, so there was no place to hide. There we were standing out in the open, with the baby dangling as bear bait."

Mike continued. "Before we could catch our breath, all of a sudden, another bear came from a different direction and went for the baby again. I scared him off with the chain saw too. The third time it happened, I began thinking a whole family of bears was after him and wondered how I was going to fight off so many bears with one chain saw. I don't know when I figured it out, but suddenly it hit me. There was only one persistent bear coming from different directions. He finally gave up and left us alone.

"I told the story to my family back east, and the next time the train came by, there was a large package for me, from Sears. It turned out to be a rifle from my dad, with a huge note on the wrapping paper that boldly said, USE THIS. And I did."

River said, "We were all grateful for your dad's gift. You can't help but worry about your neighbors out there. I felt a lot better knowing you had a gun for protection."

"Yeah, it worked out. It's amazing how the instinct to protect your children will change your passive ways."

Sharon said, "I guess bears scope out the weakest targets or easiest food, looking for the path of least resistance, in this case a helpless baby." Then she thought about how the demon bear at the cabin had gone for her first. River was out in the open, but the bear had cornered her.

"How did you and Mary come to homestead?" Sharon asked.

Mike said, "Same as most people out here. Disillusioned with society. We met River in 1972, right after he came up. I came to Alaska in 1971 and spent my first winter in Anchorage. I'm from Michigan and that spring we came up to stake out land and he had just come from New York to do the same thing. He was about five miles from me, so that made us neighbors. There was a camaraderie between the people staking out land, all of us doing the same thing, living out a dream."

"What was the dream?" Sharon asked.

"Live off the land, get back to nature, and be self-sufficient. River was kind of the same way. He liked the outdoors and all that. His dream was to build a log cabin with an axe. So he builds this whole cabin—I mean felling the trees—and everything with an axe, just because that was what he wanted to do. You know, it was an opportunity for all of us to do what we wanted. It was a glorious time."

Mike continued, "Now, River's cabin was up on a ridge, and my cabin was north of there, up a creek. I never did the dogsled thing, though. I got around on snowshoes and skis. Didn't like dogsleds, because I can't stand the barking dogs. They howl all night, chew on each other and poop all over. You have to clean up after them, feed them …"

Mary, River and Sharon were laughing hard, and agreeing that it was all so true.

"I'm serious. When you're going down the trail behind the sled, it's fantastic, but the first time they see a moose and take off through the bushes after it, they just about kill you. You have to cook them food ..."

"We get the picture, Mike," River said through laughter and tears.

"I also didn't like snowmobiles. They're better now, but back then you'd get out miles away and they'd die on you, and then you're out there with a match, trying to clean the spark plugs, sucking on the gas hose—forget it. But snowshoes, now, they always work.

"River brought a black Labrador retriever with him, and he was a good sled dog. Plus River trapped. I was never a trapper. I was pretty rough and green. But, it's easier to survive in the wilderness. You know you'll get to eat, and don't need much to survive, but in a busy city, they frown on you shooting birds or squirrels out of their trees."

Everyone agreed. Then there was a knock on the door. Mary and Mike both ran to answer, while Sharon and River looked on, confused at their sudden spurt of energy. The door opened and in walked Peter and Ginny Stanley.

"Oh, my gosh," said River, as he leaped across the room and Ginny gave him a bear hug. Sharon had never met the Stanleys, but had heard many stories about them.

"I can't believe you're here," River said over and over, while shaking Peter's hand.

Mary and Mike were standing by, beaming, as if they had materialized the Stanleys themselves. River asked, "Did you know they were here?"

"Yes. They came by the office today, looking for you, and needed a place to stay."

"You've got to stay with us," River insisted, and then realized he had not introduced them to Sharon.

"Sharon, these are our dear friends, Peter and Ginny Stanley."

"What a pleasure," Sharon said. "You are definitely invited to stay with us."

Mary invited all to sit down and relax, but everyone was talking at once and no one was listening. Finally, they calmed down, settling in the living room and began to renew old friendships.

All agreed they had loved living in the wilderness, although each had eventually moved to town. The Stanleys' town was back in Virginia.

Mike said, "When we first moved to Talkeetna, we rented a small place near the visitor's center and liquor store. That building used to be the post office, and there was an old guy named Major Kirkman, who was the postmaster. Hated guys with long hair, and he was an old drunk. He claimed to be the one grouch Talkeetna purported to have. He actually liked being called that. I would go into the post office to pick up my mail, and there was a counter that held all the pigeonholes for the mail."

"Mike," Sharon said, "River told me about him, but I thought he was making it up."

River beamed as he smiled. "I don't make stuff up."

"Sure, you don't. He told me this story about how he was looking for a cable across the river, and when I asked him what happened next, he responded, 'I died.'"

"Okay, okay. So, I exaggerated a little for effect," River said.

After the laughter subsided, Mike continued. "Anyway, back to the grouch. I could look in the general delivery box and see a package with my name on it and I would say: 'Any general delivery for Mike Stewart?' And he'd say, 'Nope.' I knew he didn't like me, because I had long hair, but figured it was because he was always drunk, so I'd ask, 'Are you sure?' And he'd say, 'Yep.' and I'd say, 'Could you look?' And he'd say, 'Nope.' Sometimes I had to go back two or three times to get my mail."

"Hey, we remember him," said Peter, "He liked me because my hair was short. What happened to him?"

"Don't know for sure. He died or someone killed him over a package, and then they moved the post office."

The laughter filled the air again.

Mike said, "Everyone knew that I was no woodsman. I had never cut down a tree. I had never built anything. I spent a week packing things up to our original cabin and took the chain saw out of the box and read the instructions."

Everyone burst out laughing, which surprised Mike, because he was being serious.

"No, I'm serious. But it's about survival. Survival means staying out of the elements long enough to stay alive and having food to eat. If you get right down to it, that's all there is to it. If you enjoy doing that in a real basic way, then you live in Alaska. Most people could survive if they didn't give up. Learning to enjoy and love the lifestyle is the trick. Once you reach that point, it becomes great."

Everyone nodded and Sharon thought how good it felt to be around such special friends. It was nice to hear about something besides bears. She was just beginning to take a sip of water when Mike asked, "So, Sharon, how are you handling being married to a legend?"

Sharon almost sprayed her water and Mary admonished Mike for asking such a question, but Sharon defended him by saying, "No, really, it's okay … he just caught me off guard. I was still thinking about what he was saying regarding why people want to live such an extreme lifestyle."

"He likes to catch me off guard, too," Mary enlightened her.

"The way I see it," Sharon explained, "there is a great explanation for how I feel that comes from an old movie called, *Guess Who's Coming to Dinner?"*

"Really?" River asked, suddenly interested and leaning forward.

"Yes, when the daughter introduced her new fiancé to the family, she explained that he was going to be a famous doctor, and since she would be his wife, that would make her famous. So, if you think about it like that, by marrying a legend, I guess I have become one also."

"Great answer." Mike turned to River and said, "She's a keeper."

"I know," said River.

Mary winked at Sharon. "You know, living in nature has taught me that each day is precious and there are warnings against wasting a single one." She stood up and proceeded into the kitchen to clear the table and put away the leftovers. Sharon and Ginny followed with more dishes.

Sharon was amazed at how easy it was to talk to Mary and Ginny, and felt as if she had known them all her life. She felt it was safe to talk to them about something that was on the forefront of her concerns.

"You know, I've thought about the question Mike presented. I thought about it often, and especially before our marriage vows. Like, how does anyone live with a legend? Living with one in the making might be easier, because you are part of everything. But to fall in love with a man, and discover he is more than a man to others in that they rely on him, and he makes it possible for them to feel their life is more than the ordinary. Then how does that affect him, because in reality, he is just a man."

"Wow, you really have thought about it," Ginny said.

"Yes, I have … then he marries a woman, not part of that fairy tale. So, how does it work? Where does she fit in, and how does he stop being something he no longer wants to be, which is why he chose her in the first place? Whether he is tired of it, or wants to move on, he finds himself slipping back into the role because it is all he knows, plus it is comfortable. But, he is beginning to face his own mortality, and as a legend, he can escape it for a little longer.

"And she, who is me, begins to think or feel that she is losing a big part of who she is, getting swallowed up in this whole legend thing. So I pull away some, which scares him, and he embraces the old ways a little more, which scares me.

"I'm sure everyone can see this happening, but no one knows what to do about it, or they don't want to mention it, for fear that the dream might come to an end. I'm trying desperately to be part of his legend, because I know that by agreeing to share his life with him, I accepted everything, and that by marrying a legend, I became one, only it's easier to say than do. By joining his life, I feel like I'm giving up some of who I am. Does that make sense?"

"Totally," agreed Mary and Ginny.

Then, Ginny added, "Believe me, every woman experiences the fear of losing her identity. It happens when we marry, have children, and when the children go to school and leave home, or when our spouses become ill or die. Our outside identity keeps changing but doesn't get lost. We are still who we are, inside. We just adjust, because we can, and that's what women do."

Mary agreed and continued along the same line. "Seems women today want to compete with men in every aspect. Out here, women do as much as men. They are strong, hunt, split wood, carry felled logs, and then, once in a while, we get to take a bath, put on a pretty dress and wear makeup."

They laughed and Sharon said, "I can't believe you said that about bathing. River told me he only bathed once a week, maybe, out there."

"It's true," Mary agreed. "It was a lot of work to take a bath. I like living in town better. Don't get too hung up on the legend thing. Every person has some legendary experiences, and the good thing about River is he has never gotten a big head."

"That's true. I think his faith has kept him humble."

Sharon quickly said, "I'm not sure if I would call him humble."

When the laughter calmed down, Mary said, "Relationships are beautiful, but a lot of hard work, no matter who they are or where they take place. How good are you at counting numbers when you get mad?"

Somewhat confused, Sharon answered, "Pretty good, why?"

"Nothing special. Just learn to count." And Mary winked as they rejoined their husbands, who lit up like Christmas trees when they walked into the room.

# Chapter Twenty-One
# Wilderness Choices

Before the women came back into the room, River quickly brought Peter and Mike up to date on the dangerous bear encounters. The three men immediately began plotting against the two bears. All agreed something had to be done soon, but how to do it without accident to themselves was something that needed to be well planned. Careful strategy, as complete as the Devils Canyon run, was an absolute necessity. Trouble was, River had years to prepare for the canyon, but only hours to get ready for this, and who knew which would prove to be the most dangerous?

"Plus we were a lot younger then," Peter said.

"But, hopefully, we are a lot smarter now," said Mike.

They laughed and River thought about how much his life had changed over the years. In the past, visitors had come to hunt big game in Alaska. In earlier years, River would transport some of these hunters and help them accomplish a successful hunt. It didn't take long to realize that this type of head hunting was not what he was about. River would much rather take a sport fisherman out to catch wild salmon or rainbow trout and turn them loose, than to kill a grizzly bear for someone's wall.

He developed a philosophy toward nature that involved look, see, and share the world. He still occasionally hunted wild game meat for personal sustenance, because he considered this to be healthier than the store-bought meats, but to kill for the sake of killing was not part of his sense of what was right.

River had spent two weeks learning the absolute feel of the boat on the river before Devils Canyon, practically living on it because every craft is different, and he needed to react in the proper way. He tried to get this point across to other boat pilots in training, because if they took the time for the thought process to take place of what to do next, it would be too late. They had to be reactive. There was no time to think. River trained them not to think, but react properly.

It would be the same when tracking The Big One. There would be no time to think. The plan came down to Peter, Mike and River going after the bears, no matter how long it took. Israel would stay and manage the business affairs.

Fortunately, business had slowed down a great deal with the end of the season at hand. River was trying to decide how to run interference with Sharon, when she discovered what he was up to. They could stay in touch by cell phone. Someone had to call in reinforcements, if necessary.

Mike thought about the massive responsibilities River shouldered. He had an amazing talent for driving boats; it was like a second sense. The talent carried over in the business world, in dealing with clients, juggling schedules, employee troubles, and boat breakdowns. Mike loved working for him, but would not want to be in his shoes. He could see why Sharon was frustrated. Why was it that River always had to solve or fix everything? Everyone pulled together, but River was constantly at the helm. It was just the way it had always been.

"Peter, can you be ready early in the morning?" River asked.

"I'll be ready," he responded.

Mike asked, "Do you want me to bring my chain saw?"

They laughed, and River said, "I don't think we want to get that close."

"Probably not. I'll take care of getting the boat ready and making sure Israel covers the office. We only have one tour tomorrow, so you two can sleep in and get your beauty rest. What time do you want the boat ready to go?"

"Say, 6 a.m. That way, Sharon won't be up yet."

"You aren't going to tell her, are you?" asked Mike.

"Nope."

"I think you're making a mistake," Mike said.

"You know she would be scared to death, or worse, insist that she go with me. I'm glad Peter and Ginny are here. Ginny will be with her, and can keep her from packing up and leaving me when she figures out where we are. When I saw that bear go after her yesterday, I couldn't react—I was too worried about her. You know, if we hesitate, we could get hurt."

"You're right, because those bears won't be hesitating. They'll just be attacking," Peter said. "How do we find them?"

At this moment, the women came back into the room, and the mood changed to carefree. The planning would have to wait. Amazing how women lightened the load of life, just by their smiles.

"River, did you ever tell Sharon the story about the firewood dispute?" Mike asked, hoping it wasn't obvious he was trying to change the subject. He was not good at being deceitful, so getting River to tell one of his long, involved stories would help to keep Mike from blabbing to her about what was going on.

"Uh … no, don't think so. Did I, honey?" River wasn't good at lying either.

Sharon had a feeling they were hiding something from her, but said, "No, and if it is about a bear, I don't want to hear it."

"Okay, you're safe," said River, grateful to be able to jump into another subject. "No bears were around that night. But a lot of erratic behavior was. I don't think Peter or Ginny have heard this one either. It happened after they left."

"I don't think we have," Peter agreed, a little too quickly, and they settled down to listen to yet another one of those amazing tales from the Mahay journals.

River began, "These two guys got in an argument over firewood, of all things. Like we don't have a million trees out there."

"One was Hank, who lived in a cabin on Clear Creek and did part-time jobs in Talkeetna, even occasionally working for Mahay's doing some general mechanical work. The other was Bill. He, along with his wife and child, lived on a trail about three miles from Hank. The nearest road system was approximately nine miles away. We didn't know it at the time, but Hank was a schizophrenic. He carried a Ruger Super Blackhawk .44 Magnum, and was very practiced with it."

"Why do you always know the full names of the weapons, but not the individuals?" Sharon inquired.

"Because that's the important stuff," River said, winking at his bride. "Anyway, Hank had a dispute with Bill over something that amounted to nothing and decided to cover the three miles over to Bill's property, and cut firewood with a chain saw in front of his cabin.

"So he was in the process of cutting the wood when Bill came out of the cabin, with his wife and 12-year-old daughter in tow. When he saw Hank, Bill confronted him by saying, "What are you doing cutting firewood in my yard?"

"Hank didn't answer, but pulled out a .44 Magnum and shot Bill without warning, once in the stomach and once in the hip, from eight-feet away. Bill went down, but unbeknownst to Hank, Bill had a .45 Colt under his coat in a shoulder holster and he was a good shot. Bill pulled out his gun and tried to shoot, but the gun jammed. Hank, seeing this, got wide-eyed and panicked. He nervously tried to unload the remaining four shots into Bill, but hit erratically in the dirt around Bill.

"In the meantime, Bill managed to clear the jammed gun and put three carefully placed bullets around Hank's heart. Of course, Hank went down, too. Bill's wife and daughter witnessed this whole event from just a few feet away. Seeing both men down, and dying, they ran back into the cabin, and called over the CB radio to Talkeetna for help. Immediately, the emergency medical service was contacted and a Trooper helicopter was dispatched."

Thirty minutes later, River lifted off from Talkeetna in a trooper helicopter. They had two medics, the pilot, and one Trooper on board heading to the scene. The flight was short, and knowing the country well, River acted as a scout in finding the exact location of the cabin in the remote wilderness below. After spotting the cabin, they then tried to locate the spot where the men were down.

When the call first came in, it had been said there was a shooting with two people down, but did not specify whether the shooter was still at large or not. Hovering over the cabin site left them exposed to ground fire if a shooter was still in the area. They spotted a clearing in a swamp, about a quarter mile away and put the chopper down in the clearing.

River continued, "Hopefully, we were a safe distance away to avoid getting in the middle of the shooting, and Bill's wife picked us up on a four-wheeler ATV."

They traveled the 400 yards to the shooting site, where both men were lying on the ground, six feet from each other, and both were conscious, but still had their guns next to them."

"Although Hank was near death, he recognized me. The last words he spoke were, 'I drew first blood.'"

Because of Hank's wounds, no one could believe he was still talking. The men were loaded into the chopper and taken to Palmer Hospital. There was no hope, and Hank died.

Bill had been hurt badly, also, but his body responded to medical care. Fortunately, he hung in there, and three months later, he and his wife took the medical team out to dinner. It was later learned that Bill's gut shot missed the descending aorta by one-quarter inch, which would have meant sure death. Amazing.

"The last words Hank spoke to the Trooper and me, 'I drew first blood', saved Bill from legal matters later. It wasn't that Hank was trying to be noble, he was bragging. I'm sure he didn't realize that his words saved the other guy from going to jail."

"That is amazing," Sharon said, just shaking her head.

Ginny said, "How awful for the wife and daughter to watch him gunned down."

"How were those guys still alive?" asked Peter.

"That was a mystery to all of us, but you know that unless you get a head shot you don't die right away."

The men were thinking that it was the same way in a hunting situation when trying to kill a grizzly. The instant-kill shot was generally a headshot, but the head was only about the size of a bushel basket. The skull was very thick and unless the bullet made a direct hit, it likely would ricochet off the skull. The bullet had to hit the skull directly in order to prevent the ricochet. River only knew one man who had been able to do this with a handgun. And he did it twice. It was Peter Stanley. Who better than Peter, to help track and kill the bears?

Finally everyone decided to call it a night. Peter and Ginny finally agreed to spend the night with River and Sharon.

"This has been a wonderful evening," said Sharon. "Thanks for inviting us."

"Our pleasure," answered Mary, who hugged Sharon and whispered, "Keep counting."

This was very good advice, considering Sharon would have been furious if she had been aware of the plot between Mike, Peter, and River to go after the bears in the morning.

# Chapter Twenty-Two
## River Ghosts

River pretended to be asleep when Sharon came to bed that night, even ignoring her when she softly asked if he was asleep. It would be better to avoid conversation that might cause him to reveal any hint of the plans for the following morning. She finally gave up and rolled over. He waited until he could hear her soft, rhythmic sounds of breathing and knew she was deeply asleep, before he breathed a sigh of relief.

He sneaked out of bed and went into his workshop to make sure his guns and loads were ready for the business at hand. He also needed to formulate his plan for the kill. He wanted to make sure neither bear was able to sneak up on them again. He searched his memory for anything that might help him better prepare. *Get into the bear's heads*, he thought. He hoped Peter's aim was half as good as it used to be, and he decided to also prepare killing loads for Peter and Mike's rifles.

There had been many times when he and Mike had been called out to risk their lives. Once it had been over two hunters who almost 'ate it' at midnight. River had received a call late at night from the Troopers. They said two guys from Big Lake were missing on the river. They had been moose hunting, with all their gear and guns in the raft. At some point they had grounded on a gravel bar and by the time they got off the gravel bar, it was dark.

Instead of exercising good judgment and camping out for the night, they came down the river in the dark. They had hit a fallen cottonwood tree, which of course swept them off the raft and they lost all their gear, but were able to somehow grab a second fallen tree. Their boat had been swept under a log in the Talkeetna River. Everyone was looking for them, but no one knew they were hanging onto a log, only two miles north of the place they were searching.

They had been able to save their backpacks with cell phones inside. One cell phone wouldn't work, but thankfully, the other one did, only because it had been protected in a plastic bag. It had taken 90 minutes to get a signal before they could dial 911.

Since it was fall, it was dark. When the Troopers first called River, they had asked if he could do anything to rescue these men. He walked out on the back porch of his house and looked to see how much light there was. It had been a moonlit night, but there were occasional clouds in the sky. As long as the moon stayed out, he would be able to navigate. If they lost the moonlight and the shoreline too, the search was over, or he could be injured. He called Mike and of course, they decided to go out.

Because they were familiar with the channel system, they eventually found the men, but could not reach them. A cloud had moved in front of the moon, making it pitch black. River and Mike were traveling about 40 mph, bank speed, on a channel that was only 10- to 15-yards wide. So, losing the shoreline and their bearings for just several seconds proved disastrous. River shouted, "I can't see anything, Mike! Brace yourself and hold on, we're going to crash."

That was the last thing River said, before they hit a log that had been suspended out over the water, five yards from the bank. The nose of the boat just barely cleared the top of the log, so the boat rolled up on top of it, teetered, and slid back down into the water. They ate the dash, but amazingly, they weren't seriously injured, just banged up a little.

What was even more remarkable was that the boat was still floating and all the controls still worked. That's when River said, "Mike, we can keep going or we can turn back." If you tell me you want to go on back, we'll go." He wanted to give Mike the choice, because the chances were questionable of them living through this one without injury.

Mike said, "No. Keep going." They both knew there were two lives out there depending on them. The only reason they kept going was because those guys were going to die if they didn't rescue them.

So, they went for it, and found the guys who were hypothermic, wet, and scared, but happy to be rescued. However, River broke the bad news to them: "Don't thank God yet, we're not back, not out of danger." There was no guarantee that they would make it back. The guys laid on the bottom of the boat and all four men prayed in their separate ways. Each of them knew how lucky they were to be alive. It must not have been anyone's time to go yet, because they all made it back to the dock.

About a month and a half ago, River had received another rescue call about four young rafters from Chicago that were missing on the Chulitna River. They had been described as 19-to 21-years old, wearing only T-shirts and shorts, with no safety provisions or life jackets. They had spent the day on the river, but now were missing.

Israel, Mike and River spent two hours searching the shoreline as well as all the channels, but couldn't find them. Everyone from the area knew of the dangers of being out on the river unprepared, and time was running out for the young men.

While heading back to town, River saw four guys walking down the side of the road, in T-shirts, shorts, and no shoes. They were on the main highway and River had been looking for them on the river. "What in the world? You guys wouldn't be four guys from Chicago who were rafting?"

They didn't have a clue what they had activated or what kind of danger they had been in. River figured they were dead, and if they had still been in the river, they would have.

He called the troopers and said, "Stand down the helicopters, stand down the fixed wings." All the local air taxis were standing by to try to find them. The community really pulled together big-time in matters involving life and death.

That very next night, River had received another call that two different guys in a canoe were lost. But then he had found out early on that they were safe, because they were on the shore and had built a fire. So he hadn't had to go out, thanks to cell phones. They had called in and told everyone they were safe.

Troopers had often pointed out to River that there was no money in their budget for doing this type of rescue operation. They didn't have the resources or equipment. Didn't matter. Mahay's Riverboat Service and local air taxis always stepped in.

*God bless cell phones,* River thought. *Everything gets dropped when someone is in trouble. All tours stop, and the boats are volunteered to turn to search and rescue until the situation is stabilized. It's expensive to do, but there is no price on a life in the Bush. It didn't matter if it was a boat or a plane down, someone in the water, whatever life-threatening condition arises, everything stops and everyone pulls together.*

It ticked him off when people risked their lives doing dumb things. And they risked the lives of others. River saw it happen all the time. It was amazing that more people weren't killed on the river. People didn't understand or appreciate the dangers of being on the water. He once saw a family in an 18-foot johnboat with husband, wife, and several children loaded to the gills with four inches of free board above the water. None of them had life jackets on. That thing had barely been able to move and all they needed was one big wave to swamp the boat. They didn't understand that this wasn't a bass pond or Disney World.

He had done many rescues and pulled a lot of people out of the river, alive and dead. Troopers called him because they knew about his rule to drop everything and help. Kind of like he was doing right now, with the bears, dropping everything to prevent a crisis from occurring down the road.

There were times when the would-be-rescued people didn't make it. There were quite a few, but some stuck in his craw more than others. Anytime someone died, it was bad, and each had taken a toll, but he refused to allow the experience to permanently damage him. He trusted this particular bear adventure would not either.

River suddenly felt tired and saw the ghosts of all the deaths he had witnessed on the river. There was a dad in his 70s, fighting a 58-pound king salmon for at least an hour. His dream in life was to catch a salmon in Alaska and that's how he went out. His son was with him, and they had been fishing up at Clear Creek. They were from the Lower 48, but had their own boat.

The dad had a heart attack and died. His son started CPR, and River happened to be passing when he saw what the son was doing, pulled over and did a rescue. The rescuers did the best they could, but he died anyway before reaching Talkeetna. His son had to go through the whole ordeal of getting his dad's body back home.

Then there was the ghost of Max Stevens, a river guide. His eight-year-old son was with him and four or five clients, going to Clear Creek. At Clear Creek, Max jumped off the bow, missed the bank, and fell into the water. He got caught in the anchor rope and the current pinned him underneath the boat. His son went running up to the clients, for help, but none of them would pay any attention to him. The boat slid off the dock, and was floating down the river. One of Mahay's guides saw the unmanned boat and pulled it over. He was shocked to find a body underneath. River got the call, and went down with the ambulance.

He worked on the body, trying to save him, using CPR. The man's features were distorted from the water, so no one recognized him at first. River did though and said, "This is Max Stevens."

River had seen Max's son several days later at hockey practice. He told River, "I wish I was older. I tried to tell them Dad was in trouble, but because I'm just a kid, no one would listen to me."

That was a horrendous thing for an eight-year-old to go through. The son is a fine young man today, and doing well.

The river current is always strong and can easily pin a person in debris. It was similar to the strength of the mountain and would never let up. River had been a dedicated paramedic or EMT worker for 13 years. Unfortunately, in a small town, most of the people River worked on, he knew.

The sad thing was, not many people realized that CPR rarely worked. When River trained other paramedics, he warned them not to get their hopes up too high. But you couldn't stand by and do nothing; you had to do something. So you tried.

There were memories of dozens of embedded fishhooks over the years. He kept the hooks sharp so he could push them easily through the skin when removing them. Usually, he took his knife and made a little hole to get it out, acting fast while people were still in shock.

The ghosts of children were the hardest to endure. Once he had been doing a shuttle with 10 people on board. Heading up the river, he saw a small raft turned upside down. A man and woman were standing on the shore, frantically waving. River pulled over, and learned that their 11-year-old daughter was missing in the river. They had seen her float down around the bend.

River recognized the man and woman as past clients who used to ride with him. Immediately he unloaded the passengers and took a couple of volunteers who were physically fit and willing to help. Around the corner, they discovered a large logjam. The tricky part was trying to find the young girl in the river. River crawled on the logs and looked between them, searching for half an hour, but finding no sign of her.

Finally, he went back to the place where the raft had originally turned over and noticed a little color hung up on a snag, about 15 feet downstream from the raft. The father reached over the side to grab what looked like colored cloth, and to his horror, grasped the daughter. The gas line from the can had wrapped around her ankle, holding her about 12 feet behind the boat just under the silted glacier water. She had been in the cold water for 45 minutes.

River was the only qualified individual who could do CPR, and the only one who could drive the boat. This created a dilemma. Knowing that without CPR there was no hope for the girl, he utilized the other passengers' assistance. One of the clients made a call to have the ambulance waiting, but he still needed someone to drive the boat.

It turned out that the father, who was in shock, was the only one with some boating experience. Could the dad do it? He said, "Yes." So, River gave him the wheel, and went back to doing CPR. The father was able to get the boat safely back to the landing site, where the ambulance was waiting. River went with them in the ambulance to the Palmer Hospital. Everything possible was done, but she didn't make it. Experiences like this were difficult to put to rest.

The ghosts haunted his thoughts, suddenly bringing to light another experience, this time involving his youngest son, Noah. The river had almost taken him, too. Judah was the hero that day. They were all fishing on a peninsula. The kids were playing on the quiet, shallow water safely away from the main stream, in sight of the adults fishing nearby.

Suddenly, four-year-old Judah came running up, saying, "Daddy, Daddy! Noah's in the water." Noah was two years old. River looked over to where they had both been just seconds before, and Noah was gone.

The boys had waded into the river. A wave from a passing boat had knocked Noah off balance, and the current immediately took him away. Because it was glacier water, it was impossible to see anything below the surface. Scanning the river in front of where the boys had been, River caught a faint glance of color, and said a prayer that it might be Noah. He panicked, because he had pulled a lot of dead people out of the river.

*It's got to be Noah,* he thought, *but if it is, he's all the way under.* The thought sickened his stomach as he dove in the icy waters— headfirst, grabbing at anything near where he had seen the color. It was Noah. He got him to shore but he was not breathing.

He prepared to do CPR, but Noah started coughing, spitting out water, and crying. It was one of the most frightening experiences of River's life. If Judah hadn't said something, or if River had hesitated for even a half second, Noah would have been gone. It was too close. So many memories permeated his mind.

Another ghost invaded. River began working at six in the morning, and continued until 11 at night. He covered 200 miles of remote wilderness on any given day. He frequently ran into people who weren't familiar with what they were doing on the river, and got into trouble.

He was going up to Clear Creek, and was almost there when he came across two guys in a canoe, fishing at Dolly Hole. He was only 100 yards away when he saw their canoe flip over.

River had four people on his boat. Two of them were in the military, and also very fit. During this time of year, the water temperature was around 40 degrees, and a person in the river had only a few minutes before becoming hypothermic. The cold water could drain all the body heat in five minutes or less.

River was fully aware of this fact as he watched one guy make it to quieter water, and pull himself out. The other guy was about 220 pounds, in his late 20s, and very fit, but he was swept downriver. He instructed the two military personnel to get the life ring and throw it to the guy as they reached him. They got the life ring to him, and tried to pull him into the boat, but he was too heavy and they couldn't lift him over the side. River instructed the would-be victim to hang on to the life ring and be towed to shore. But he was unable to hang on because of advanced hypothermia.

At this time, River was faced with the dilemma of having to land a two-ton boat on the shore while fighting a 10 mph current, without crushing the victim, because they still couldn't get him in the boat.

At long last, he was able to put the boat on the shore, and they pulled the man out of the water. He had been in too long, and his speech was slurred. He was still in danger.

River called 911 and jetted back to the dock to a waiting ambulance. Upon arrival, the victim received full life support and was taken to Palmer Hospital.

Three days later, he came back and shook River's hand for saving his life. They weren't all sad stories. Recalling this rescue always raised River's spirits and gave him hope.

By now he had the loads fully prepared and ready to go. There was one thing left to do to prepare for the hunt. Probably the most important thing—sleep. He headed back to the house, being quiet so as not to awaken Sharon—then slid into bed and quickly went to sleep.

# Chapter Twenty-Three
# The Hunt

River had the car loaded with the hunting and camping gear by the time Peter joined him at 5 a.m. He had also cooked up a cornucopia of savory foods in his favorite iron skillet to make sure they ate a hearty breakfast before heading upriver to hunt bear. He was as excited as a little kid going on a fishing trip.

Peter was also excited and impressed with the breakfast spread. "Wow," he said. "I had forgotten about your famous breakfast meals." A delectable aroma filled the kitchen and his eyes were large with delight. There in front of him, sitting on the table was a beautiful cuisine smorgasbord of moose meat, scrambled eggs, fresh orange juice, wheat toast with real butter and jam, and several different kinds of fruit. He suddenly noticed the baker's rack against the wall in the dining room and said, "I see you've added to your iron skillet collection. How many do you have now?"

"A bunch," River smiled from ear to ear. "You can never have too many iron skillets. Everyone needs iron to be healthy."

They ate in silence, concentrating on the flavor and texture of each bite. After his appetite was satisfied, River said, "I've got our gear in the car." Peter helped clear the dirty dishes, then scrape and load them in the dishwasher. River didn't want to give Sharon one more thing to be ticked off about, like a messy kitchen.

"That's something different," Peter said, pointing toward the dishwasher. "I thought you were never going to use one of those contraptions."

"I wasn't, but guess we all change, and they do come in handy sometimes," River said. "Especially when you're in a hurry."

"What about the leftovers?" Peter asked.

"What leftovers? The girls have to eat, too." They laughed.

"Good thinking." They put the cooked foods in the fridge, ran out the door, jumped in the car and headed for the dock. The packed supplies consisted of two sleeping bags, a tent, backpacks, skinning knives, proper survival gear, food for sustenance, salt for the hides and two sets of binoculars. Mike would bring his own gear and it was a sure thing that he would already be on the boat.

They arrived promptly at six o'clock. Just as River suspected, Mike was there, and had the boat fueled up and ready to go. They decided to head toward Clear Creek since this was the best feeding area for bears. River had counted 13 bears there just last summer. It was a popular gathering place for the bears because all their favorite foods were plentiful there: Salmon, blueberries, and cranberries. *Learn their habits and get into their heads,* River thought.

They would scout the ridgeline from the boat for about a 10-mile radius, because that was the most probable distance a bear traveled, if food was available.

River's old cabin, where one of the bears had almost attacked Sharon, was the last known sighting, and was built on a well-traveled bear path, but the feeding areas were about four miles away. A grizzly could easily cover four miles quickly. It was unlikely that the bears would return to the cabin, but it would be a good place to set up camp. Besides, Peter wanted to see the cabins again. River also wanted to check for bear paw prints to compare them with the one he measured on the boat, to see if he could identify that it possibly belonged to The Big One or Demon.

River's cabin was built on a ridge and bears frequently traveled the ridges. They liked to be high and then drop down to the food in order to feed. A good hunter, whether human or animal, always watched for movement. Animals didn't have the best eyesight, and River was often surprised by how close a moose or mink passed by him, almost stepping across his feet, as long as he stayed very still. More often than not, if the hunter didn't move, the animal would not see him.

River was concerned about identifying the exact bears they were hunting. There were distinguishing marks on certain bears, and it was particularly difficult to recognize bears from a distance. These two were large, but other than that, it would be tricky to be sure they had the right ones.

Once there had been a bear in the area that people named "Three Toes." At some time in this bear's life he had been caught in an illegal bear trap, so he only had three toes. His paw print was easily identified.

Going back to the cabins to find identifying prints was probably a waste of time, but if they didn't spot the bears while scanning the ridge from the boat, they would head to the cabins to take a look around. Besides, it would be more comfortable staying there, and Peter was anxious to go.

Hopefully the way to find The Big One or Demon was to cut the engine and drift the river near the shoreline while scanning the ridgeline with the binoculars. It was long and tedious work, but had paid off in the past when hunting bears for food.

It was beginning light when they jumped into the boat and headed upriver. Peter had been excited to see his cabin again, but not under these circumstances. It had been too many years since he had been in Alaska. He said, "You know, there is one constant out here, one thing that hasn't changed a bit. There is never a boring minute and you never know what you're going to find. Bored is not part of Alaska's vocabulary. I just showed up to say hello, and here I am going with you two, to trap a couple of wayward bears."

River and Mike laughed. "That is amazing, isn't it? We're glad you showed up," River said.

"Okay, this is the area we should expect to spot some bears."

They cut the engine and started to drift. The men took their binoculars and scanned the ridgeline, as planned.

"Peter," River said, "I once asked Mike this question, regarding a river rescue, and now I'm asking you both. We can keep going or we can turn back, now. If either one of you tells me that you want to go back, we'll go. I want to give you the choice, because this is risky. We are looking for two huge grizzlies. At least one of them, and maybe both, has no fear of man, has tasted man's blood and has the killer instinct. That makes him more dangerous."

River was always concerned for the safety of others. He couldn't make Sharon understand that when he was alone, he didn't feel any risk, but when someone was with him, he was apprehensive. Having Mike and Peter along was a huge asset, but he wanted to make sure they were completely comfortable with the decisions being made to hunt these bears.

"You know my answer," said Mike. "It's the same as always. I'm here to help do whatever needs to be done. The way I see it, this needs to be done."

Peter said, "My answer is the same as Mike's: We keep going. Seems to me there are lives at stake and people depending on us. We have to keep going because someone, maybe even one of our own family members, might be hurt if we don't deal with these bears. I'm just glad I can help."

"That's all I wanted to hear," said River and they continued searching the ridgeline. They were getting close to the place where The Big One had last been spotted when River's cell phone began ringing.

"Uh, oh. Guess who it is?" River asked.

"I imagine it is your lovely bride? What a great tracker she is. Maybe we should have brought her."

The men laughed nervously and River answered the phone.

"Hey, Sweetheart."

"Hey, yourself. Where are you? And don't try to lie to me because I've already heard the truth. I talked to Ginny and Mary. It's amazing to me that their relationships with their husbands are based on honesty. I just want to know one thing."

River knew better than to say anything until she was done venting.

"Do you have a death wish? Because if those bears don't kill you, I just might finish the job."

*Whoa,* River thought. *She is angrier than I've ever seen.*

"Why are you doing this?" Sharon continued. Then she was quiet. "I don't want be a widow and I don't want to live here anymore. I'd rather be married to a coward who's alive and has some common sense, than a foolish dead hero."

Uh oh. He had been afraid she might pack up as soon as she realized where he was and leave for New York without him. He had hoped that having Ginny there would keep her home until the deed was done. *Remain calm,* he thought. "Honey, just trust me on this one, okay. I promise you everything will work out."

Sharon didn't answer for a long time and finally she said, "Are Mike and Peter with you?"

"Yes. They're both here."

"Well—that's good." Sharon seemed to be calming down knowing the three of them were together. She realized there was nothing she could do, so resolved to cool off. "Just be careful, okay? I guess I'll probably still be here when you get back. But we've got some trust issues to talk about."

"Okay. You're right," River answered. "Thanks, honey."

"I'm not very rational at the moment. I'm furious. So, don't push your luck. Please look out for each other. Be safe. Oh, what's the use? Goodbye." Sharon hung up.

"Whew," River said. "That went well." He laughed, not because anything was funny, but because the tension level was high, and everyone on the boat could feel it. As a matter of fact, Sharon's stone-cold voice and words enveloped the boat and dampened his disposition like a soggy blanket. There really was no logical reason not to have told her the truth about what he was doing. This was just something that had to be done. He realized that he had been more afraid of facing her than Big Bear. He laughed at his reference to the name she had given to The Big One.

When he had left the house in the early-morning hours, he felt guilty not discussing his plans with her, but if he had, she would have insisted he not go, or worse, that she go with him. He had to go, and rationalized that he couldn't react properly when she was with him, because he would be worrying about her safety. Realistically, she was probably more ticked off because Ginny and Mary knew the truth and she was the only one left out of the plan. He hadn't thought about that before.

Peter having showed up was a blessing. She would eventually agree, he hoped, that it must have been meant-to-be. Peter was talented with a rifle and handgun. They also all had their cell phones, he laughed, and everyone was aware that cell phones saved lives now in crisis situations in the wilderness. There were three of them ready to make a call for help in case a rescue was needed. The emotional temperature of this noble quest, however, had now changed for the worse, because of Sharon's phone call.

"Told you to tell her," Mike reminded him, and they burst out laughing relieving the tension that had built. Mike had a way of making him laugh.

They got back to the work at hand, and scanned the area for over an hour. They spotted several black bears and small grizzlies, but none were large enough to be the bears for which they were searching.

"Okay," River said. "What do you say we tie up the boat in the exact place Sharon and I left it two days ago? I didn't tell this to anyone, but when we picked up my boat, there were huge paw prints inside. I measured them and got an idea of the print that might be The Big One. Based on the size, I'm fairly sure they were his."

"Really?" Mike was surprised.

"Yep. I've made the grizzly loads, too. Why don't we take our gear up to Peter's cabin?"

Peter and River loaded the guns. Each had a handgun and a rifle. They were literally loaded for bear.

"I'm also pretty sure I saw The Big One watching the boat yesterday close to this area when I was returning from Devils Canyon."

"Really?" Mike and Peter were surprised again.

"If I didn't know better, I'd say he does seem to be following you," Mike said.

"It is strange," agreed River. "But I'm sure it's just a coincidence. I've been in this area a lot lately."

They reached the shore, tied up the boat and started their hike with the gear to River's cabin. They would later move on to Peter's cabin. They each wondered if they were being watched. They wouldn't have to speculate for long.

Chapter Twenty-Four

# Trouble

Back at home, Sharon wasn't sure if she was more furious because River didn't have enough faith in her to discuss his plans, or just because she was completely frightened of his getting hurt, or worse. *River had not lied to me, per se,* she reasoned, *but running off to track The Big One, knowing how I feel, was nothing short of ... well ... untrustworthy. Why would he do it?*

She wondered when Ginny would come out of the bedroom so she could vent, and tried to read, but couldn't concentrate. She turned on the television, but wasn't able to focus. She grabbed some of the food Peter and River had left in the fridge, but wasn't really hungry.

*I wonder how long it takes to massacre a couple of huge grizzly monsters,* she thought in anger. It was fortunate for River that Sharon did not realize they could be gone for days.

*Maybe I should go to work,* she considered, but didn't want to be in the office, for fear of discussing what River, Peter and Mike were up to, and then being responsible for worrying everyone else. All she could do was pace the floor and wait to see what happened next. Just like all the other wives in the world who knew their husbands were doing something dangerous, though noble.

River, Peter and Mike have to be scared, though, she thought and took comfort in the fact that there were three men against two bears. The numbers had to work in their favor.

*I hate Daniel Boone,* she thought. *Why couldn't my husband have a hero like Shakespeare, someone who stayed inside where it was safe, and didn't go around feeling responsible to rescue the whole world?*

Sharon decided to watch the Devils Canyon video again. Maybe watching him accomplish what others had failed to do could make her feel better, and instill confidence in her that he would succeed against the bears. Besides, watching the video over and over, helped her learn more about improving her personal presentation to the tourists on the Devils Canyon tour, that is, *if* she decided to stay in Alaska. And, at the moment, that was a *big if*. *It's no big deal*—she tried to convince herself, *I'm sure he's done more difficult things than exterminate two giant grizzlies. At least I hope he has, anyway.*

Ginny walked into the living room and discovered a very distraught Sharon who was overly excited to see her.

"You're up!" Sharon practically shouted.

"Yes. What a comfortable bed. Thanks so much for asking us to stay with you," Ginny answered, but then noticed that Sharon seemed a bit on edge and her voice cracked when she spoke. "Are you okay?"

"Yes and no," Sharon answered honestly. "I'm worried about the guys looking for bears, or more about the bears looking for them."

Ginny's demeanor bothered Sharon when she realized that Ginny did not seem to be distraught. "Aren't you worried?" she asked.

"Yes, I am," replied Ginny. "But the three of them working together make a very powerful team. I think the bears should be more worried. They are all superior with guns, and although older, I think age has made them more cautious. They have seasoned well, you know." They laughed.

"I hope you are right. Sometimes I think River has a death wish."

Ginny was surprised to hear Sharon say that, because River was one of the most level-headed and capable men she had ever met. "I really don't think you have much to worry about. They'll be fine."

Ginny pointed to the television screen and asked, "Are you watching a movie?"

"Trying to. It's the Devils Canyon video. It reminds me that I'm married to Superman and he can't be harmed, unless it's kryptonite, and not by bears. Do you want to watch it with me?"

"I'd love to," Ginny replied, glad for the distraction, and hoping to cheer Sharon up. "But do you mind if I grab some breakfast first?"

"I'm sorry. No, of course not. The men left a feast." They went into the kitchen to eat and to get to know each other, wondering what made each other tick. They never went back to the television. There was too much to talk about.

"I hope we get to see the boys while we're in town," said Ginny.

"Judah isn't here," Sharon said. "He's in school in Michigan, but Israel and Noah are, so you should be able to see them. You know, because I don't have kids of my own, I love having three handsome stepsons."

"That is a good thing," Ginny agreed. "I love having three sons, too. That's another one of the many things our two families have in common, plus we all love Alaska."

"Alaska is easy to love. Did you know that The Big One is one of three sons, too?" Sharon asked.

"Really? How do you know that?"

"I don't know for sure. River and I are only surmising that The Big One was one of the three cubs in the tree in front of your cabin where River shot their mother."

"I remember that. It's interesting that you both think that," Ginny said while reminiscing about the time when River had killed the grizzly sow in front of their cabin door while they were visiting family in Virginia. "So, do you think the bear is out for revenge?"

"No we don't, and that is the oddest thing. It seems as if he has some kind of affinity for River; they are connected in some strange way. When Big Bear saved my life yesterday from the Demon Bear, he followed us for a distance and had stopped next to that same tree in your yard. River saw him standing there watching us. I really don't think he is out to hurt us, on purpose, but that Demon was a different story."

"That's funny how you've named the bears," Ginny laughed.

"True," Sharon agreed. "But giving them names makes them a little less ominous to me, which helps to keep me from being scared stiff and running screaming all the way back to New York."

They laughed, and Ginny pointed out that it seemed Sharon was doing just fine living in Alaska.

"Thanks. I do love it here, but would not have lived out in the wilderness as you all did."

Sharon remembered that Peter and Ginny had a "normal" life back in the Lower 48, but chose to come to the wilderness. She took this opportunity to ask a question that she had been mulling over in her mind.

"Ginny, why did you live out there in the wilderness, with children, no less, giving up your creature comforts, when you didn't have to do it?"

Ginny smiled and simply said, "I didn't know I had a choice."

Sharon contemplated the difference between she and Ginny, then stated, "I *know* I have a choice."

"You're right. We always have choices, and I was only joking. If I had to choose one favorite thing about living out here, I think it would be the whole family-togetherness experience. I loved our wilderness home as much as Peter and the boys did."

"Really?" Sharon said, "I'm not sure what my favorite thing about Alaska would be but one of the highlights of my new quasi-wilderness experience happened the other day when Judah called to ask my opinion regarding a personal matter. I felt needed and it was as if I finally belonged here. I really miss my friends, family phone calls and visits."

"I remember that was difficult for me, also," Ginny agreed. "It's not easy making new friends or building relationships with a ready-made family and having to prove yourself all over again. But it does seem you are making great inroads."

"I hope you're right. I do love River and the boys. They usually refer to me as their father's wife, and not stepmother, but recently Judah said, albeit jokingly, 'Listen to your new mother.' I melted, right there on the spot. I guess the ages of the boys make a big difference in the way they have welcomed me into the family. Since they are older, they are more secure within themselves, and were okay with giving me a tiny space in their hearts."

"You are probably right. Knowing how much you love their dad probably helps them feel good about your marriage. Along with seeing River happy."

Suddenly remembering the crisis at hand, Sharon admitted, "I wish I was more secure at the moment."

"I'm sure it will all work out," Ginny said.

Sharon envied Ginny's confidence and said, "River and Kris did a fantastic job raising the boys."

"They did, but living out here is almost cheating, in a manner of speaking. It's just easier when your family is part of everything you do. And you're together because there's nothing else to do. You have to rely on each other. It's an amazing way to raise children. The whole experience provides opportunities for building character."

Sharon laughed and said, "And I have met many characters here."

Ginny also laughed and had to agree. *It didn't matter where you lived,* she thought, *relationships were always the most important thing.* She felt sad that River and Kris were no longer together, but it was easy to see why River had married Sharon. He certainly had good taste in women. The Mahays had played an important role in the Stanley family's wilderness adventure. The rugged lifestyle had formed friendships that would last forever.

She didn't let on that she was also worried about the men tracking the bears. Peter was a little rusty with a weapon, Mike had always been against using guns, and River must have been more concerned about the dangers if he had felt the need to keep what he was doing from Sharon. She didn't seem to be the type of woman who couldn't handle doing what needed to be done.

There had been a lot of dangerous situations, but they had gotten through them all. Obviously, even short visits continued to offer opportunities for risk and concern. She recalled a time when their middle son, George, had found himself in serious trouble, and been lost on the river. He loved to hike and explore, so came for the summer to spend time at his parent's Talkeetna cabin. He had been hiking out in the Bush and decided to take a new route back to Talkeetna that he had never taken before.

He had been following what seemed to be a well-used trail toward the Talkeetna River, but soon discovered that the trail disappeared right into the river. Then he realized the current path was nothing more than a winter snowmobile trail.

To backtrack would take several days, but if he followed the river downstream, he hoped to eventually find a place to safely cross. Unfortunately, the route down river turned into a vast swampland where he lost direction and wandered in circles for the rest of the first day. Cold and wet, with no food, he had made a dry camp for the night.

The next morning, he continued to search for a way out of the swamp but kept coming back to the river's edge. He crossed small river braids that led him to a series of swampy islands. At no place did the river itself allow any chance of crossing. At the end of the second day, he realized that he might have to spend another cold wet night in the swamp. With no food, and hypothermia creeping into his body, he knew time was running short. He had to get out.

At long last he heard a familiar sound in the distance. A jetboat was heading upriver. He rushed to the shoreline, but it was too late. It had already passed, but George knew that what went up the river, had to come back down.

He had little strength left, so he made a decision to wait on the shore however long it would take for the boat to return. After several hours, just before nightfall, he once again heard that beautiful sound of the jetboat returning. He waded into the shoals of the river, frantically waving his arms in the air and shouting for the boat to stop.

What a surprise to find that it was River driving the boat. He was returning from dropping off supplies upriver, and was just as surprised to see George, who he recognized immediately as being in danger. He was walking into deep water and could have easily been swept away, especially in his weakened state. Fortunately, George moved back to the shore and was rescued. What a great reunion. To this day, George swears that River saved his life, but as usual, River says he was just in the right place at the right time.

Ginny smiled and said, "You know kids in the Lower 48 seldom have the opportunity for the kinds of experiences they could have in Talkeetna and other remote areas of the world."

Sharon said, "I can see that, and I've heard Israel say the same thing. Did you know that he plays an integral part in the business and actively participates in the day-to-day operations as a boat captain? He does a lot of the driving."

"I had heard that Israel was working full-time in the business. My sons, who have visited Talkeetna from time to time, told me about his successes on the river. Seems like father, like son."

Israel had often told Sharon how he felt pretty fortunate to have been raised in Talkeetna, and also that it had been a blast growing up in a family business. "It sure worked for me," he said. He gave the credit for his personal work ethics to this good fortune.

Sharon thought about the stories of Israel's younger days, when as a 12-year-old he had exemplified a desire to have more fun and do fewer chores. He and his friend Brennan, who was Sandi Mischenko's son, were assigned the job of cleaning the boats at the end of the day, around 11 p.m. It was still daylight, but no one was around, so they were always playing. There were many fun distractions for young boys to do when no one was looking over their shoulders. So, they didn't clean the boats, and River fired them, but Kris would hire them back and tell them to sneak back to the dock and clean the boats.

"Do a good job," both moms warned, but then a couple days later, they'd get fired again.

At age 13, they had a brilliant idea to take the emergency flares off the boats and light some to see what they looked like. Signal flares, when handheld, will spew out a 10-foot cloud of bright orange smoke, so when someone was in distress they could be seen many miles away.

The boys lit one, and quickly realized their cover might be blown because the flare was doing exactly what it was designed to do; attract attention. They decided to get rid of it before they got caught and fired again.

They threw it in the outhouse by the dock, thinking that would put it out. Unfortunately, it didn't work, because seconds later the outhouse looked like a fish smoker out of control but instead of wood smoke it was puffing out huge clouds of orange flare smoke.

Next, they decided to throw water on it and grabbed buckets of water from the river, ran to the outhouse, and dumped the water on the flare. This didn't work either. Eventually, the flare burned itself out, leaving the inside of the whitewashed outhouse a bright-orange color.

Sharon knew Ginny was correct about living in Alaska. If that had happened anywhere else, the boys would have gone to juvenile detention, but their punishment had been to clean the now-orange outhouse, which was no easy task.

Sharon laughed and Ginny asked what was so funny.

"I was just thinking about some of the funny things I've heard that the boys did when they were little," Sharon answered. "I think you are right about living in Alaska. If some of those escapades had been done anywhere else, the boys would have been in trouble with the court system."

"That's true," Ginny agreed.

Ginny and Sharon were having so much fun getting to know each other, and were so deep in conversation that they were startled when the phone rang. It was Israel calling from the dock.

"Sharon. Mike called and said to let you know that they were all doing just fine and on the way to see Peter's cabin."

"Really? Well that is good, I guess. Thanks." *I wonder why River didn't call me,* she thought.

Suddenly, Sharon heard several angry voices over the phone. Israel was arguing with someone.

"Israel, what's going on?"

"It's Chet Bastian again. We just got back from today's last river tour and Bastian is down here with a couple of his flunkies annoying the tourists by passing out fliers that bad-mouth Mahay's."

*Oh no*, Sharon thought. *Don Lee's warning had come true.*

Israel took one of the fliers and read it quickly. "This paper says that we're destroying the environment with our boats and don't care about anything but a profit, because we put lives at risk on the river. Now they're shoving those papers at our clients who look pretty up-set. I gotta go, Sharon."

"Israel. Don't fight him," Sharon pleaded. "Try to get the clients away as soon as possible."

"I'll try, but gotta go. Bye."

Israel hung up. *That awful man,* Sharon thought and explained to Ginny, "An unpleasant man named Chet Bastian is down at the dock bothering the clients. We heard he was going to do something like this yesterday, but he didn't. Poor Israel. Come on. I'll tell you more on the way."

Ginny quickly followed Sharon out the door. Sharon drove as fast as possible while giving the details about Chet Bastian. "He is jealous of River and the Mahay business, and always threatening to cause trouble but has never really done anything, until now. This time he's stepped over the line.

"Everyone at Mahays, and especially Israel and Noah, have had just about enough of his rude comments and accusations. I'm afraid this time Israel might be pushed over the edge and exchange physical blows. What an inopportune time for River to be out in the woods playing with bears."

Ginny had to agree that the timing wasn't very good.

They arrived at the dock, just in time to see the last tourist trying not to take the flyer being shoved at him as he boarded the bus. Usually people who completed a tour were laughing and chattering about the day's experience, but this individual looked apprehensive and perturbed.

Finally all the tourists were on the bus, and Israel started walking back to the boat, but Chet Bastian was following in hot pursuit. It was obvious that Israel was maintaining as much control as possible, and working hard not to make a scene in front of the tourists. Bastian wasn't making it easy.

"Uh oh," Sharon said. "I'm afraid there is going to be a fight."

She parked the car and raced toward the dock with Ginny close behind. Israel suddenly had had enough and grabbed the flyers and threw them all over the parking lot. Then he walked out on the dock.

Chet Bastian, of course, was furious and followed Israel. Seeing this, all the fury and frustration that had been building up inside Sharon reached a boiling point. She ran between them and said succinctly, "Everyone needs to cool off." She turned to Chet Bastian and said clearly, "Get off our property."

Sharon's words had a sobering affect on both men, who froze for a few seconds, not sure what to do next. Israel glanced at Sharon and Bastian seemed to take advantage of the distraction and lunged toward him.

Sharon stepped forward to come between them, and accidentally hit Bastian with the full force of her shoulder, knocking him off balance. He fell into the shallow water with a splash.

Everyone was in a momentary state of shock, but the bus driver broke the spell by starting to clap. The passengers on the bus joined him. A very wet Chet Bastian climbed out of the river and onto the shore. He glared at Sharon and walked to his car, where he and his buddies jumped in, slammed the doors and sped out of the parking lot.

Sharon said, "I didn't mean to do that." She figured she had ruined any chance for River to have an amicable conversation with Chet in the future.

"I'm glad you did," said Israel. "Guess he learned not to mess with our family."

Everyone busted out laughing. Ginny said that Sharon was to be crowned the next *Mountain Mama*. The bus driver opened the door and all the passengers ran over to congratulate her.

"I didn't mean to do it," Sharon insisted, but was proud of Israel's comment. She was feeling pretty good about the way things worked out, when suddenly she saw another boat coming toward the dock. Mike was piloting this one, and he was alone.

*Oh no,* she thought. *Where were River and Peter? Were they hurt? Were they still alive?*

# Chapter Twenty-Five
# Another Legend

River and Peter were hiking up to the old cabin, with guns ready. Their eyes scanned the woods, watching the trail for evidence of recent bear activity. The proof was apparent. Occasionally, River knelt down and put his hand on the ground where the brush was crushed, to see if it was still warm. There was no way of knowing if the two bears they were after had been the ones recently on the trail.

River was grateful Peter had decided to visit Talkeetna again at just the right time. Peter was well-known for his use of a handgun. He was the first person River had ever known to have killed a bear with one shot from his handgun, and he had done it twice. This took a tremendous amount of skill, as well as a steady hand.

Peter pointed out that before he had come to Alaska, he spent many days practicing at the shooting range. He had known that he was going into the wilderness where his ability with a handgun could make the difference between life and death.

It was obvious that many times a rifle could be left leaning against a tree, or on the boat, or someplace else other than where it was needed. A rifle was cumbersome and not easily carried, as a man went about the daily chores of living in the wilderness. A handgun, on the other hand, could be holstered on your side, always ready within seconds, if needed.

Peter fired the gun so many times, he wore out the barrel, which took as many as 20,000 rounds to do. This was the same gun he later gave to River, after having the barrel repaired to good-as-new.

Peter was fully aware of the magnitude of the dangers to be faced, and that was why he wanted to develop his skills with the .44 Magnum. When River and Peter first met, they would go shooting together. River was amazed at Peter's ability to put the bullet exactly where he wanted it to go. This skill proved to save his life and the lives of others many times.

River had killed a number of bears since he had come to Alaska over 30 years ago, and each one had been as difficult as the first. They were magnificent animals, unpredictable and capable of surviving at the top of the food chain in the untamed wilderness. They were as dangerous as the river, and you could never let your guard down. To do so could be death, and many had experienced this. *Better safe than sorry*, River reminded himself. *Don't think, just react.*

He recalled a time when a bear's appearance in his backyard in town, had put at risk his three sons who were playing outside, and at the very young ages of six, four, and two. Their village cabin was on a half-acre lot, with virgin woods all around, and unlike the wilderness cabin, they enjoyed running water, electricity, and even an inside bathroom.

One of their neighbors, Marie Jackson, was a retired lady in her 60s who lived alone in a house next door. Marie had left the upstairs window open, because it was a warm, sunny day. While she was gone, a bear climbed a tree, and went right into her bedroom.

When Marie returned home, she discovered a bear on the upstairs balcony looking down at her. She obviously became very agitated, nearly hysterical, and immediately ran to the Mahay's home. This behavior startled the bear and he turned to run out the same window he had come through, then down the tree near where the boys were playing in the sandbox, only a stone's throw away. Fortunately, at the last moment, he suddenly veered away from the boys and ran up another tree.

River grabbed the boys, took them into the house and returned with his rifle, joining several other neighbors also carrying rifles who were standing around looking up at the bear in the tree. A younger lady from California, new to the neighborhood, argued that bears were cute and it was imperative to figure out how to get rid of this bear without harming it.

Another neighbor, with similar beliefs as the lady from California, and obviously not aware of the danger of bears, took matters into his own hands and ignorantly threw a rock and hit the bear. Now, this really ticked off the bear, and before he could maul someone, while everyone was arguing about what needed to be done, River resolved the issue. He quickly shot the bear.

No one except River was willing to do the extreme amount of labor required to prepare the meat, so he and his family ate the bear. Most hunters didn't realize it was easy to pull the trigger, but the real time-consuming and hard work took place after that.

*End of that story*, River sighed, and pulled his thoughts back to the work at hand.

Glancing over at Peter, he suddenly had second thoughts about Peter joining him on this mission. It had been a long time since Peter had carried a gun. Wasn't really necessary or even appreciated in Virginia.

They arrived at the first cabin and Peter was shocked at the damage done by the bears. "Man, this is really trashed. How bad is mine?"

"Not as bad," River replied. "You don't have as much stuff left to mess up."

They hung around for a short period of time, watching each other's backs, feeling they were being observed, but nothing they could put their finger on. Nothing happened, so they decided to head over to Peter's cabin. He was anxious to see it after all these years, and took the lead.

Peter was still in good physical condition and practically ran the short distance to his cabin. At this exact moment, River answered a cell phone call from Mike who was down at the boat preparing to carry another load up the trail. River asked if he needed help. Mike said no, that he was bringing up the last of their gear. They were assuring each other that there were no bears sighted and debating about calling the wives to let them know all was well.

Mike said he would gladly make the call, but explained he wasn't anxious to deal with an angry Sharon. That is hazardous duty, he pointed out. River had to agree and they hung up.

In the meantime, Peter disappeared between the trees, while River was distracted with his phone call. All the men were separated. An excited Peter arrived at his old cabin, forgetting about the potential danger. As he headed toward the cabin door, he glanced at what he thought was a 55-gallon oil drum. He wondered how anyone could have gotten that huge drum up there, and more importantly, why was it there?

Suddenly, the "oil drum" stood up on its hind legs. From the size of the bear, Peter was sure it was either The Big One or the one Sharon called Demon. He glanced behind him, hoping for backup, but River and Mike were nowhere to be seen. Looking back toward the bear and noticing the way the bear was sizing him up while growling and shaking it's head, Peter decided it was going to attack.

Not wasting any time, Peter fired, hitting the bear in the chest. Peter was rusty and didn't place his shots as well as in the past. This bear was huge. He turned directly toward Peter, and seemed to know exactly where that bullet came from. Now he was really ticked off and charged.

Peter fired again, hitting him in the neck. The bear shook a little, as if stung by a bee, and kept coming. The third shot hit him in the shoulder, and he shook again, but it didn't slow him down either. He was still coming.

Peter fired the fourth shot, and the bear slammed down on his stomach, and tried to get up to continue to charge. With only one round left, Peter knew there was no place for him to run if the bear got up.

He finally placed the fifth shot into the bear's immense head, and by the grace of God, it killed him. Peter realized what an incredible close call this was and his hands began to shake. The bear was finally dead, but only with Peter's last well-placed shot.

Holding an empty .44, and not having time to calm down, Peter suddenly saw another bear charging from the same direction the first bear had come from. He frantically began reloading his revolver.

When River heard the shots, he broke into a sprint toward Peter's cabin. Just as he crossed over the bluff, he saw that Peter was distressed. He immediately noticed the downed bear on the ground, with Peter trying to reload and another bear coming toward him.

Arriving at Peter's side, River attempted to take aim on the second charging bear, when all of a sudden the bear stopped its charge and stood up on his hind legs, as if studying the situation, taking in all the details. River felt as if he had stepped back in time. Here he was at the same cabin and under the same tree where 30 years ago, he had killed the sow with the cubs.

He realized once again that this was his opportunity to make the kill as he had done before, and prepared to fire while the bear was standing. Much to his surprise, something inside wouldn't allow him to pull the trigger. There was something familiar about this bear, and River knew at a gut level, they were not in danger.

Peter was completely shocked that River wasn't taking the shot. He watched in disbelief, frantically trying to reload. Time stood still as the bear towered near River, who kept the aim of his rifle steadfast on the bear. Each waited for the other to move. It was as if these two were communicating telepathically and sharing thoughts.

Finally, the bear dropped back to all fours, turned and slowly meandered off into the wilderness. Peter watched in disbelief as River lowered his gun and called out, "Goodbye, Big One."

Mike had missed the whole adventure and went back alone to the dock to get a couple of large coolers to transport the meat of the downed bear.

A worried Sharon could not be convinced that nothing had happened to River or Peter. She and Ginny insisted on going back with Mike to see for themselves.

Everyone talked a mile-a-minute bringing Mike up-to-date on the Chet Bastian incident. Mike told them about the huge downed bear that Peter shot.

"I've never seen such a large bear," he said.

They tied off the boat and helped Mike pack in the two large coolers. When they finally arrived at Peter's cabin, Sharon and Ginny flew into their husbands' arms.

With tears of relief Sharon asked, "Is it over?"

River hugged her tightly and said, "It's done. You know, I still believe that The Big One is one of the most beautiful and breathtaking creatures I have ever seen. I had my reservations about killing such an animal, especially after he saved your life."

River smiled as Sharon quickly studied his face and replied, "You believe he saved my life, too?"

"I think it is possible, and you need to know that I didn't kill him. He walked away, without incident, after Peter shot Demon Eyes. I sincerely believe we won't see The Big One ever again."

"How can you be so sure?"

River didn't answer, but Sharon knew he was right, because she knew that River understood the need of both man and animal to live freely, each drawing their strength and power from the Alaska wilderness. Her husband was a man as big as all of Alaska, a living legend because he embraced the hardships, and lived with kindness as well as courage. He would always appreciate and protect a compassionate heart, and both he and Sharon had clearly witnessed these qualities in The Big One.

That was the last sighting of The Big One anywhere in Alaska. Many wondered what happened that day, and to them, this story is nothing but a bear tale. Others who have looked into the heart and soul of the participants, as well as their own, have touched a level of awareness few mortals ever experienced. For in this interaction between man and the Alaska wilds, we find meaning far greater than conflicts between man and beast. It is where we find ourselves and the meaning of our existence, as well as that realm where fact is often stranger than fiction.

For all practical purposes, all bears are wild and could care less about humans. River was careful not to anthropomorphize any wild animal, because to do so would be foolish. Yet while nature shows no compassion towards anything in the Alaska wilds, who can say what is evolving within and among us? Perhaps once every 2,000 years, nature manifests itself, leaving all that it is to become a living, breathing entity that can interact with humans. If dogs, dolphins, and other mammals can interact positively with humans, why not a wild bear like The Big One?

These ideas would later give River many nights of deep thought and contemplation, and emphasize how much we are all connected to the natural world, rather than just a species who might carelessly misuse this God-given dominion over the earth.

As River drifted off to sleep, he took comfort in knowing that whatever the truth waiting to be discovered, there wasn't a better place to learn it and feel connected with nature than in his beloved Alaska.

(above) River Mahay never tires of sharing his world of fishing.

River is always excited with the landing of each fish, and here lands a rainbow trout.

(top left) River landing a silver salmon for a young lady. (top right) Panning for gold on Iron Creek, a tributary of Talkeetna River. (center) River Mahay loves to share his Alaska with the world. Here, River instructs a new angler in how to land a salmon.

(top left inset) The author's daughter, Nikki, is taught by River how to correctly fire a pistol. (top right inset) River's first boat, damaged beyond repair. (top center) This is a stretch of the canyon where an individual named Leo scratched his name on

the rock to which he clung. River Mahay rescued the capsized riverboater. Leo survived. (center) Sharon Mahay learning to fire a high-powered rifle. (lower) During each spring breakup on the Talkeetna River, there are many icebergs to dodge while taking clients on excursions.

*(left) River Mahay scouting water conditions to prepare for his Talkeetna Canyon run.*

*(center) A victorious River Mahay in his canyon boat, the Kristine, after successfully running the Talkeetna Canyon.*

*(bottom) Newspaper article in 1992, regarding River Mahay's victory in being the first to jetboat up the treacherous waters of Talkeetna Canyon.*

BILL ROTH / Anchorage Daily News
Steve Mahay shortly before his run upriver

# Rapid transit

## Guide is 1st to jetboat up treacherous waves of Talkeetna Canyon

By GAIL RANDALL
Daily News reporter

THE TOILET BOWL — On Tuesday, Steve Mahay became the first person to jetboat up Talkeetna Canyon — miles and miles of rolling gray water that has defied all such attempts in the past.

"It was not that easy," Mahay said after his effortless-looking 75-minute ride up the river that had only been kayaked before. "I was fighting it with each rapid."

It was the second such stunt for the 43-year-old Talkeetna river guide, who in 1985 became the first person to jetboat through 11 miles of notorious Devil's Can